FINGERSTYLE JAZZ GUITAR SOLOS

PLAYBACK+
Speed • Pitch • Balance • Loop

To access audio visit:
www.halleonard.com/mylibrary

Enter Code
3134-8257-4122-4585

For more information on Sean McGowan visit:
www.seanmcgowanguitar.com

ISBN: 978-1-4950-8354-9

Visit Hal Leonard Online at
www.halleonard.com

Contact Us:
Hal Leonard
7777 West Bluemound Road
Milwaukee, WI 53213
Email: info@halleonard.com

In Europe contact:
Hal Leonard Europe Limited
Distribution Centre, Newmarket Road
Bury St Edmunds, Suffolk, IP33 3YB
Email: info@halleonardeurope.com

In Australia contact:
Hal Leonard Australia Pty. Ltd.
4 Lentara Court
Cheltenham, Victoria, 3192 Australia
Email: info@halleonard.com.au

ABOUT THE AUTHOR

Sean McGowan is a fingerstyle jazz guitarist who combines diverse musical influences with unconventional techniques to create a broad palette of textures within his compositions and arrangements for solo guitar. His first recording, *River Coffee,* won the Best Independent Release of the Year Award from *Acoustic Guitar* magazine. Music from the recording has been published in Japan's *Acoustic Guitar* magazine and Mel Bay's *Master Anthology of Fingerstyle Guitar, Vol. 3*. His subsequent recordings, *Indigo* and *Sphere: The Music of Thelonious Monk*, offer compelling portraits of classic jazz standards performed on solo electric archtop guitar. *Sphere* was named one of *Acoustic Guitar* magazine's Essential Albums of 2011, and Sean appeared on the covers of *Fingerstyle 360* and *Just Jazz Guitar* magazines. His most recent recordings include *Thanksgiving & Christmas Tidings*, a collection of seasonal hymns and carols arranged for solo acoustic guitar, and *My Fair Lady*, featuring music from the classic Lerner & Loewe masterpiece arranged for solo jazz guitar.

Sean is an avid arts educator and currently serves as Associate Professor of Music and Guitar Program Director at the University of Colorado, Denver. He earned a DMA in Guitar Performance from the University of Southern California in Los Angeles and has conducted workshops at colleges throughout the country. Sean is a strong advocate for injury prevention and health education for musicians; his workshops incorporate a holistic approach to playing. A contributing editor and educational advisor for *Acoustic Guitar* and *Fingerstyle Guitar Journal* magazines, he is also the author of the book/DVD instructional projects *The Acoustic Jazz Guitarist, Fingerstyle Jazz Guitar Essentials*, and *Holiday Songs for Fingerstyle Guitar*, as well as several instructional methods from Truefire.com including *The Fingerstyle Jazz Guitar Survival Guide.*

Sean plays and endorses Brad Nickerson Custom Guitars, Henriksen Amplifiers, Grace Design preamplifiers, K&K Sound pickups, TV Jones pickups, and Elixir strings. For more information, please visit www.seanmcgowanguitar.com.

ACKNOWLEDGMENTS

Wholehearted thanks are due to Andrea Antognoni and Eamonn McGowan; Michelle McGowan; Jeff Schroedl, Jeff Arnold, and everyone at Hal Leonard; Bill Piburn; Adam Perlmutter; the University of Colorado, Denver; Eric Johnson; Frank Potenza; Alex de Grassi; Brad Nickerson; and Peter Henriksen.

Special thanks to you, the reader. I hope you find enjoyment and inspiration within this collection of guitar music.

ENDORSEMENTS

Sean's impressive style is so musical. You are transported by his selection of songs, but within the compositions is a masterful guitarist using multi faceted guitar arrangements at the same time, creating a single guitar orchestra!

–Eric Johnson

"Sean McGowan has found that sweet spot where the worlds of jazz and fingerstyle guitar intersect; maintaining the polyphonic clarity and sonorities favored by acoustic players that often get lost in the pursuit of dense chord changes and the use of flat keys. These arrangements will equally challenge and delight players of both genres."

–Alex de Grassi

"With the release of this book, Sean McGowan has spared us the formidable task of transcribing these unique arrangements for ourselves. All we have to do is savor the craftsmanship and artistry that this amazing stylist packs into his treatments of these timeless classics."

–Frank Potenza
Professor, Guitar Program Chair
USC Thornton School of Music

PRESS QUOTES FOR CDs

My Fair Lady

"Sean McGowan's playing and arranging are world-class. *My Fair Lady* delivers with beauty, imagination, and stunning technique."

–*Fingerstyle Guitar Journal*

"Sean McGowan displays broad inventiveness in the solo jazz idiom. His tone and execution are masterful. All of this adds up to a very enjoyable recording.

–*Minor 7th*

Sphere: The Music of Thelonious Monk for Solo Guitar

"*Sphere* ranks among the very best solo jazz guitar records I have ever come across. McGowan's arrangements are fresh and innovative... it is amazing to hear how full he sounds as one guitar player, adding layers of beautiful harmonies and a driving bass, never allowing the listener to miss another instrument. Right from the start, listeners know they are in the presence of greatness."

–*Just Jazz Guitar* magazine

"It's a gutsy move to cover Monk's music with just your guitar and no overdubs, but McGowan is more than up to the task. Don't let the solo guitar label fool you; he swings hard on "Blue Monk" and "Rhythm-A-Ning." Monk's classic "'Round Midnight" gets a gorgeous treatment, starting with shimmering harmonics. A true guitar showcase."

–*Vintage Guitar* magazine

"It takes a lot of brass to tackle the music of Thelonious Sphere Monk, the creative giant whose idiosyncratic piano playing and composing reshaped the sound and texture of modern jazz. And when the musician attempting this feat is a solo guitarist, well, that makes the challenge even more daunting.

On *Sphere*, fingerstyle jazz guitarist Sean McGowan proves he's up to the task. Wielding his 2003 Custom Virtuoso Nickerson archtop, McGowan tackles ten of Monk's tunes, including such classics as "Blue Monk," "Ruby, My Dear," and "'Round Midnight," as well as lesser-known pieces like "North of the Sunset."

With a slightly smoky yet ringing tone, McGowan captures Monk's signature rhythmic hesitations, dissonant close-interval voicings (which can be particularly tough to work out on a six-string), and playful use of silence and space.

When the music demands a fast run or two, McGowan rips with gazelle-like speed across the fretboard. But it's his ability to coax rich, sustaining harmony from his axe that puts him in a league with today's best solo jazz guitarists. Whether plucking waves of shimmering harmonics à la Lenny Breau or paying homage to Joe Pass by juggling walking bass lines, chordal fragments, and single-note bebop phrases, McGowan plays with a relaxed, swinging feel and ripe tone.

Here's the kicker: McGowan cut these tunes live in the studio with no overdubs, so the performances have an immediacy and energy that draw you in as a listener. Yet it never sounds like he's struggling with a passage or hurrying to get through the song without blowing a take. These tracks will satisfy both Monk aficionados and fans of solo guitar who may be new to this music. In fact, if you're in the latter camp, *Sphere* provides a superb introduction to one of America's musical icons."

–Premier Guitar magazine

"McGowan is exquisitely tasteful throughout, remaining true to the melodies while adding colorful textures, including harp-like interludes and occasional sprinklings of dissonance. There's an intimate feel to the CD that's quite appealing, and the consistency of tone and mood creates an ambience that's both lovely and luminous. McGowan has created an immensely pleasing CD, a work of art that allows both himself and Monk to shine."

–All About Jazz

Indigo

"Really stunning… a non-guitarist will never realize just how much is going on, but we guitarists will constantly ask ourselves, 'How did he do that?'"

–Just Jazz Guitar magazine

"Though he is not a household name in the guitar world, he definitely deserves to be. His sense of harmony and amazing technique are world-class. He is an inspiration to any serious guitarist."

–Fingerstyle Guitar magazine

River Coffee

"Sean McGowan is the most promising young solo guitarist I have ever heard. His first CD, *River Coffee*, paints a broad, beautiful picture of his enormous virtuosity, unrelenting musicality, playful sense of humor and remarkable knowledge of musical history. Guitarists will weep yet laugh with delight as they try to figure out what he is doing, and history will remember Sean as one of the most important guitarists of his generation."

–Tuck Andress of Tuck & Patti

"An emerging artist of considerable depth…"

–Acoustic Guitar magazine

PERFORMANCE NOTES

A Note About Right-Hand Fretting

Several of the songs in this collection utilize an extended fretting technique in which notes are fretted by the right, or picking, hand. To do this, place the tip of your right-hand index and/or middle fingers on the fretboard, just as you would your left-hand fingers to fret notes. After the note is fretted, use your right-hand thumb and/or pinky – depending on which string the note is on – to pluck the string using up- or downstrokes while holding the index finger down. The goal is to create a natural sound with the same timbre as strummed or plucked notes using only the left hand; however, you will be able to access higher notes, cluster intervals, and chord voicings that are impossible with the left hand alone in standard tuning. This technique is explored in detail in my *Fingerstyle Jazz Guitar Essentials* book, published by Hal Leonard.

All Blues

The introduction emulates the ostinato figure of Bill Evans's piano from the original version by using HO/POs on the D and G strings with the fretting hand, while the picking hand plays some harmonics, open strings, and finally the bassline by tapping and sliding on the low E and A strings. The melody and solo sections also feature right-hand fretting and tapping to create a piano type of effect and contrapuntal lines. Notice how chord substitutions are used within this simple four-chord blues form; try incorporating different structures in your own blues progressions.

Stolen Moments

To achieve voicings like Oliver Nelson's closed-voiced arrangement of horns, use the right-hand fretting technique to play clusters and the moving bassline simultaneously. In the eight-measure Intro, play the low C bass note with the left-hand thumb. The two G notes (on the 3rd & 15th frets of the E string) are to be played with the right-hand index finger. Fret the low 3rd fret G in advance, and pull off to that note from the left-hand thumb C. The higher G can be tapped with the right-hand index and pull-off to the 8th fret C. Meanwhile, the fingers of the left-hand work in tandem with right-hand fretted notes (indicated in boxes in the tab) for the four-note chord voicings on the higher strings. In measure 17, the right hand taps and pulls off the high E♭ to C melody while the m11 chords move up and down chromatically on the middle strings.

Prelude to a Kiss

Here, an Intro using artificial harmonics outlines an F♯7altered chord. Duke Ellington's elegant melody is then performed in a question-answer style, creating a dialogue between the melody and chords. For the second A section, the melody is more freely interpreted, with longer improvised lines outlining the melody and chord progression before leading into the Bridge section. Ballads can be wonderful vehicles to explore harmonic substitutions and single-note lines without worrying about meeting the tempo or time signature.

I'm Old Fashioned

I first heard "I'm Old Fashioned" on John Coltrane's classic *Blue Train* recording. When performing this, try to hold down the longer melody notes (e.g., bars 1, 3, 5) to their full value. This will create the sonic image of more than one instrument playing, and remain true to the integrity of the melody. One of the most important techniques of solo guitar playing is performing different articulations (i.e., short and long notes) simultaneously. The bassline should be fluid and smooth, while the upper melody and chords will alternate between short, staccato articulations and longer, sustained fingerings. This arrangement features a longer solo section with lots of chord substitutions. I recommend learning and studying the original chord changes (listed in the *Real Book*) and comparing the substitutions presented here. For example, the original is in the key of F major and temporarily modulates up to A major for the Bridge. In the solo sections, I keep this approach intact, but change it using A minor sounds (m. 57) and A Lydian voicings (m. 93). The end of the song requires right-hand fretting with an upper pedal point alternating against chord arpeggios.

Get Me to the Church on Time

The first track on the *My Fair Lady* recording opens with natural, sustaining harmonics imitating the sound of ringing church bells. Then, the melody is set over a D pedal on beats 2 and 4. The second A section sets the melody on top of a syncopated bassline in a Latin style. Practice this by playing each part separately and very slowly before putting them together. In the final A section, the melody is harmonized in thirds over a low D pedal (the low E string is tuned down a whole step to D). After a solo break, the first two A sections highlight a walking bassline. Listen to the track and observe the quick pull-offs to open strings to achieve a swinging movement. The open strings create a feel, rather than a discernible pitch – kind of like a drummer hitting accents against the constant time on a ride cymbal. The Bridge and subsequent A sections feature single-note lines interspersed with chords before returning to the song at the Bridge and taking it out. The ending also returns to the low D pedal bass, with chords ascending the neck, creating a tension and release between major, minor, and diminished-seventh chords.

On the Street Where You Live

A real straight-ahead, moderate-swing groove pervades this arrangement. After a short rubato Intro, the melody is presented in a two-feel, with a conversational dialogue between the melody and bassline. Try to articulate this as if there are two distinct players. This is achieved by creating a contrast in articulation between the melodic, chordal, and bass parts, like the concepts in "I'm Old Fashioned."

Confirmation

Here's a good technical challenge in playing counterpoint. Charlie Parker's bebop melody is difficult enough to play by itself, let alone over a constant walking bassline, with little chord jabs here and there. However, take one measure at a time and practice it very slowly, with a metronome clicking on beats 2 and 4. The solo is presented in a pianistic style, as counterpoint ideas and single-note lines alternate with chord voicings and bass notes. The final melody is played without a constant bassline, instead dialoguing with quick chords for a different texture. The Intro theme returns after the final melody before launching into an improvised solo cadenza, essentially over Gm7 and C7 chords, and resolving to F major.

Polka Dots and Moonbeams

Jimmy Van Heusen's beautiful song features quite a few reharmonizations. I decided to arrange this melody in a somber, poignant mood by contrasting the diatonic melody in F major over highly chromatic and dissonant chord voicings. The movement from Dm7 (vim) to B♭m6 (ivm6), as in Wes Montgomery's timeless version, is one highlight of the original progression. I kept that intact and elaborated with a diminished-third cycle (B♭m7-Gm7-Em7) in mm. 36-37 and 72-73. This arrangement is an experiment in creating different colors and moods with constant structure, pedal tones, and common-tone voice-leading between otherwise unrelated chord structures.

My Romance

One of my all-time favorite standards. This setting includes a lengthy introduction that utilizes extensive right-hand fretting, starting in measure 15. The picking pattern is the same in that the right-hand thumb arpeggiates the low E up to B string and the pinky plucks the high E string, all while the right-hand index and middle fingers fret notes on the A and high E strings. This effect creates a harp-like sound, plus unique voicings not possible with the left hand alone. The melody displays rhythmic freedom, and stays close to the original chord changes. There are moments of artificial harmonics and single-note passages in the styles of Lenny Breau, Joe Pass, and Earl Klugh. The song concludes with a nice chordal ending featuring a lot of constant structure to create contrast in color, yet harmonic unity with the add4 voicings.

There Will Never Be Another You

This is another moderately fast swing arrangement that alternates between a two feel and a four feel in the bassline, and an overall contrapuntal texture between the bass, chords, and melody. There are several solo choruses here, alternating between single-note phrases outlining the changes as a horn player might, balanced with a more pianistic approach by adding chords and bass notes. Playing with different rhythms (eighth- and quarter-note triplets) and phrasing over the bar lines can add another dimension to your soloing and keep things interesting in a solo guitar context.

Ruby, My Dear

Thelonious Monk's "Ruby, My Dear" is a masterpiece, recognized as one of his most beautiful compositions. The progression is unique and fun to play over, so I decided to do two choruses with some solo improv – not just one time through as I often do when playing a ballad. Monk's tunes challenge us to evoke his feeling through chord voicings and phrasing, and to add something singularly personal. After recording an entire album of Monk's music, I discovered his style fits surprisingly well on the guitar – many of the voicings and chord progressions flow quite naturally on the fretboard. For the solo section, I opted for a contrapuntal dialogue approach, creating the sound of two different soloists playing off one another. I also tried to stick with Monk's theme of ascending chords in the ii-V sections as anchors to hold down single-note excursions. The melody is restated in a higher register after the Bridge, before ending with extended-fretting chords – to emulate Monk's picturesque harmonies.

Where or When

Another favorite of mine from Rodgers and Hart. The lyrics and chords have a mystical feel to them – simple but very deep. To capture this enigmatic feeling, I used an alternate tuning of CGDGBE, low to high. This works well, especially for ballads, as it creates a cello-like sound with the low three strings in fifths; however, the top four strings are tuned in standard, so common chord voicings and intervals are still recognizable. As with most of my ballad arrangements, I added little sections here and there in the form of introductions, interludes, and outros. I hope you enjoy working through this setting, and that you will be inspired to explore this alternate tuning in your own music.

All Blues

By Miles Davis

A

*Chord symbols reflect basic harmony.

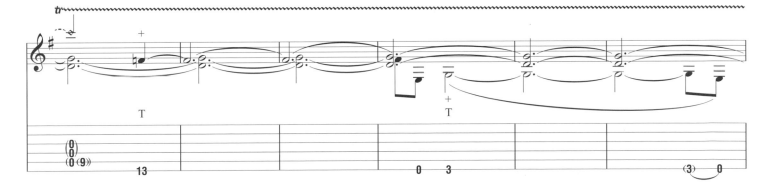

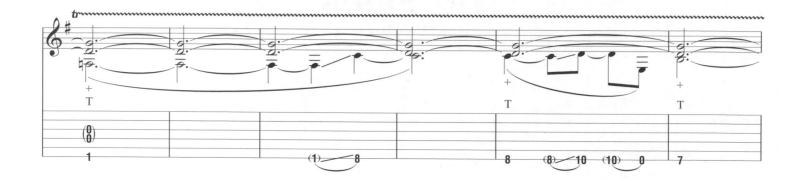

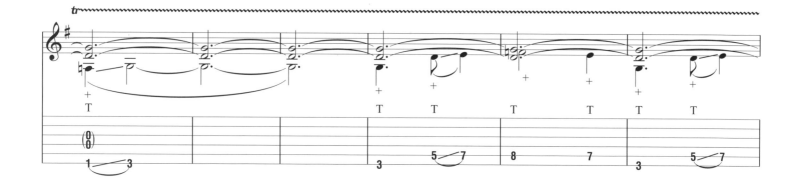

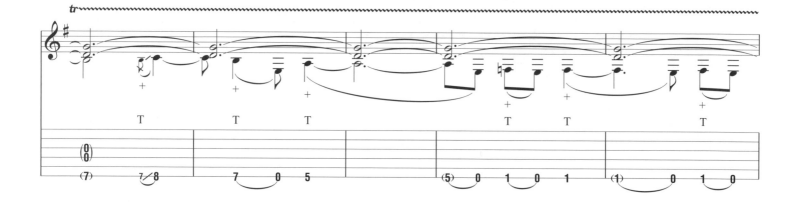

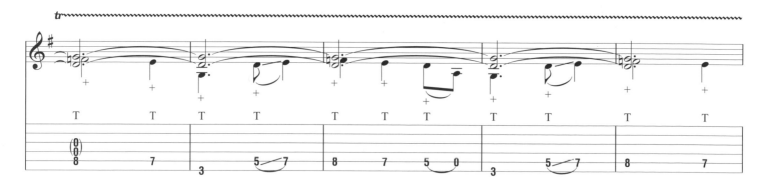

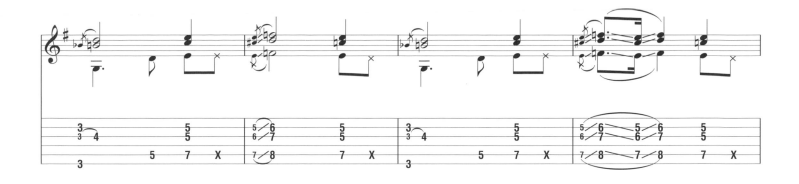

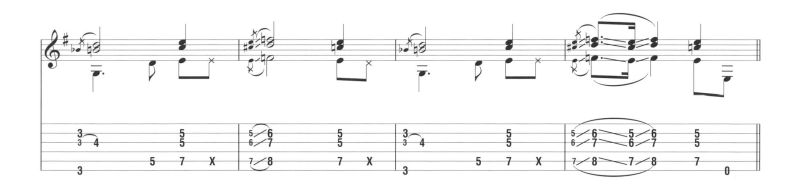

B

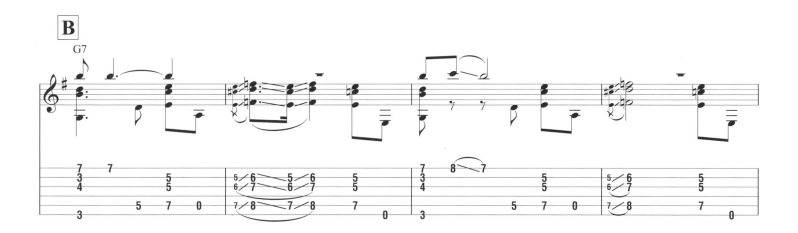

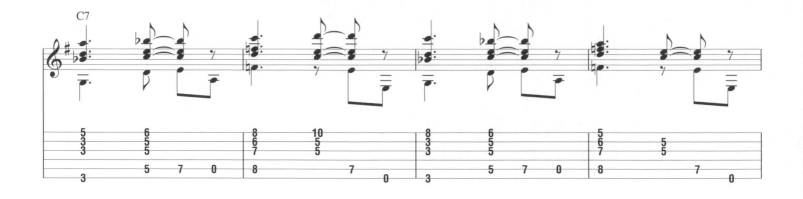

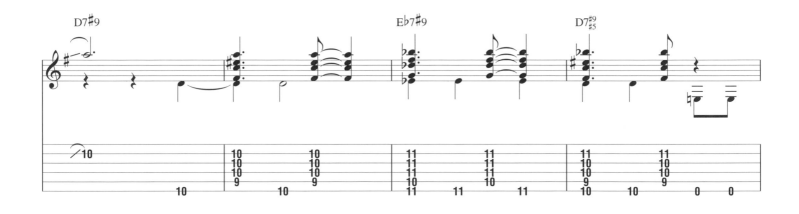

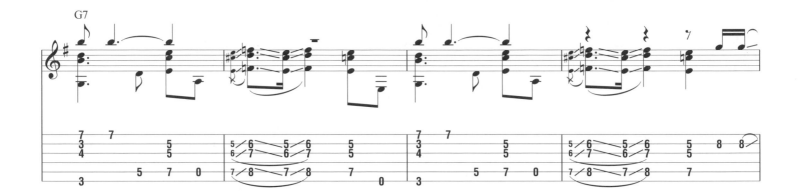

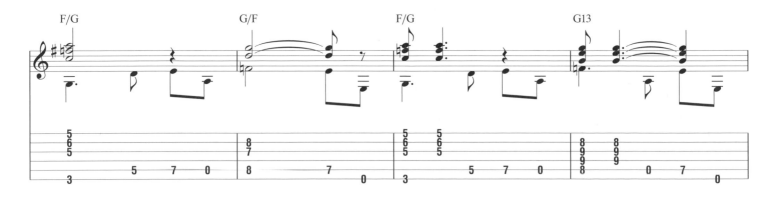

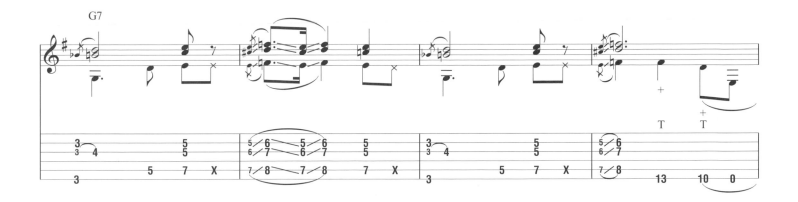

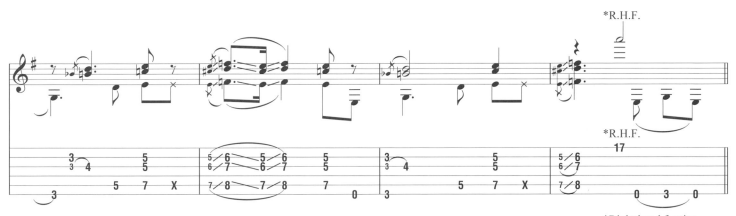

*Right hand fretting
(see Performance Notes).

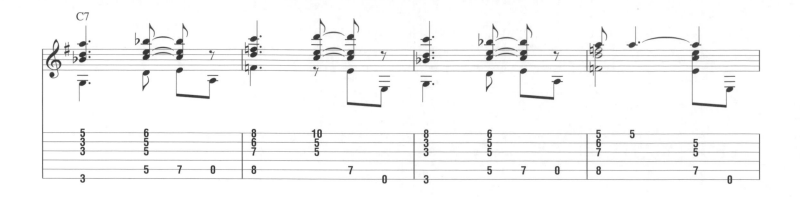

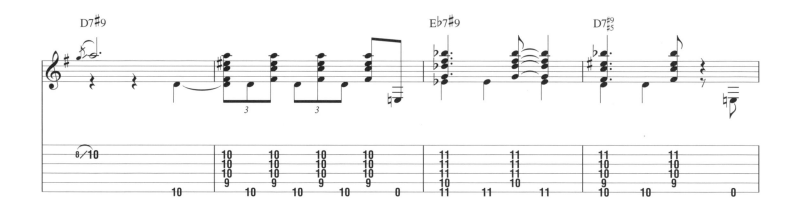

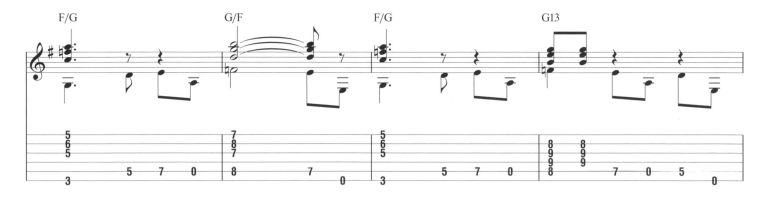

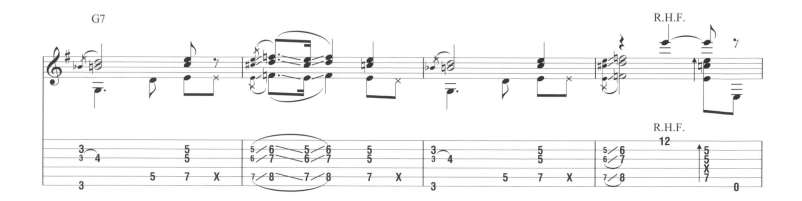

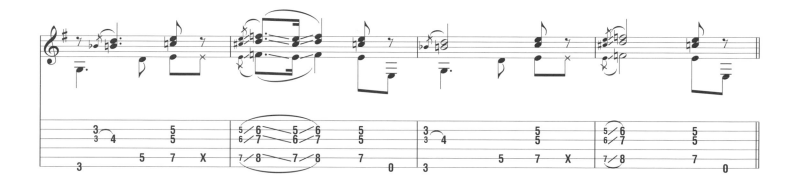

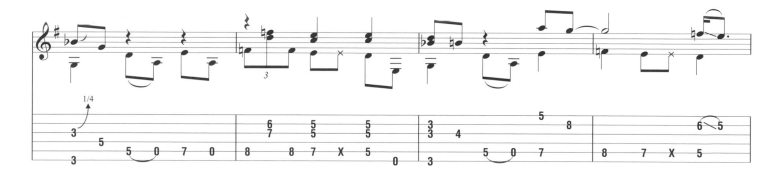

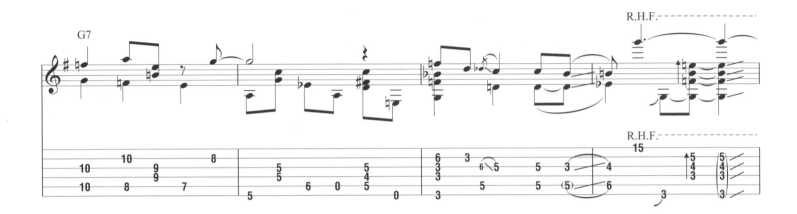

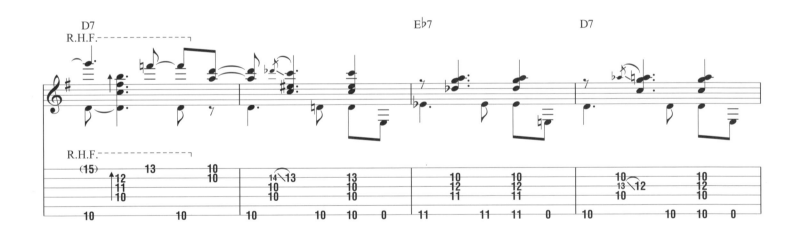

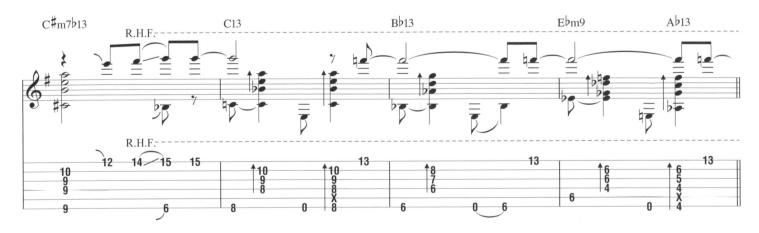

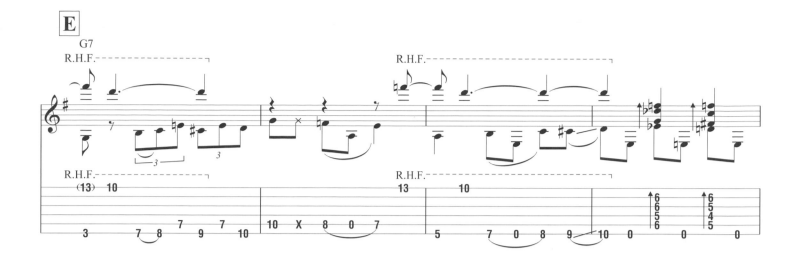

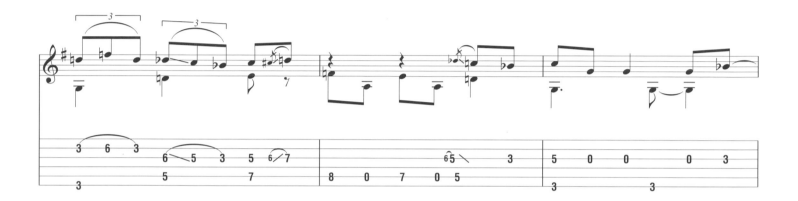

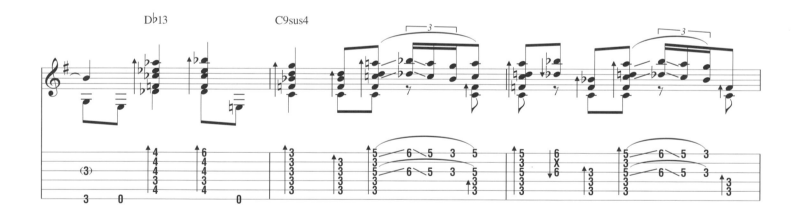

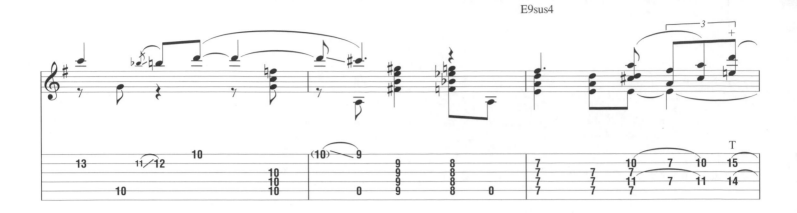

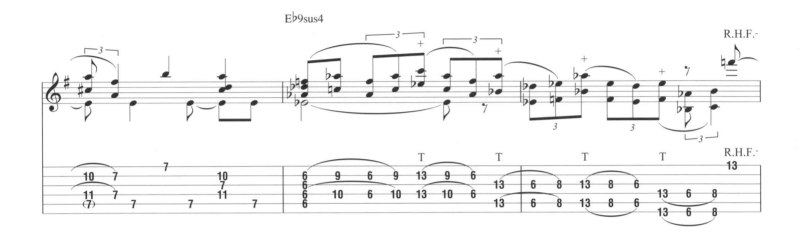

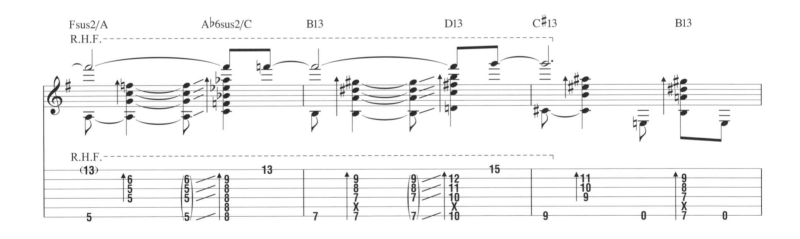

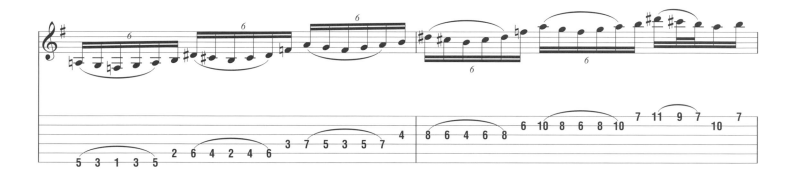

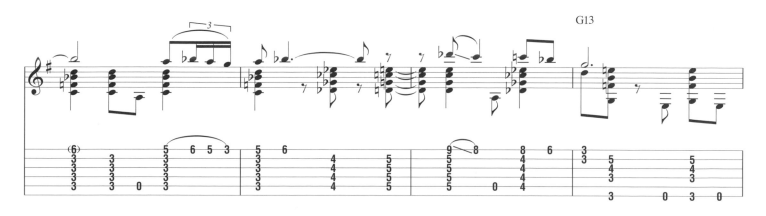

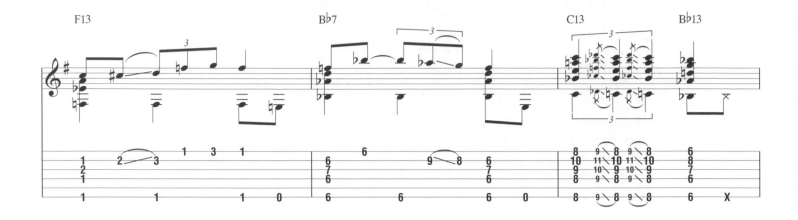

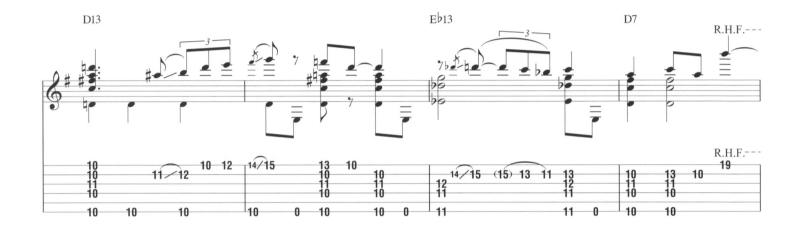

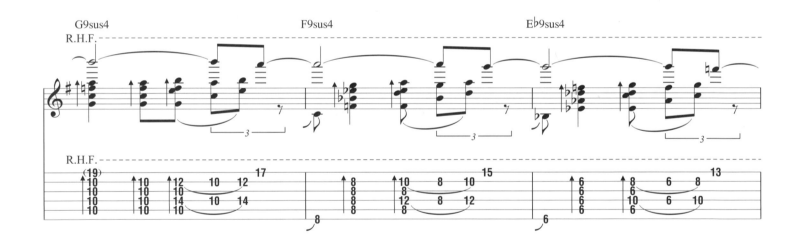

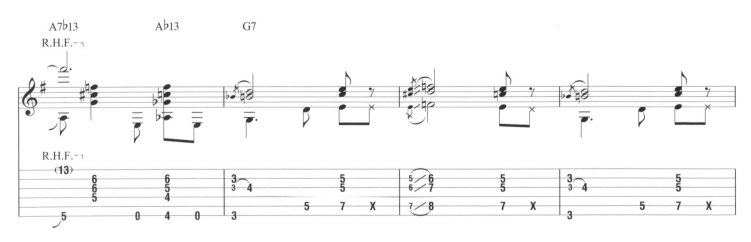

G G7

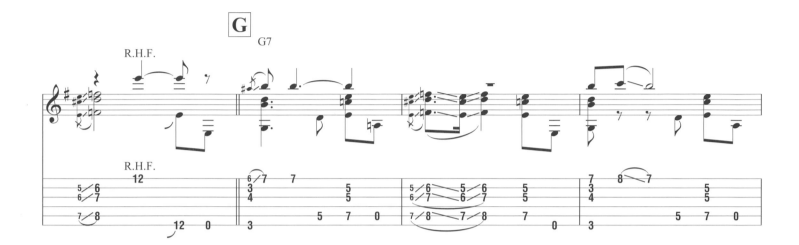

C7

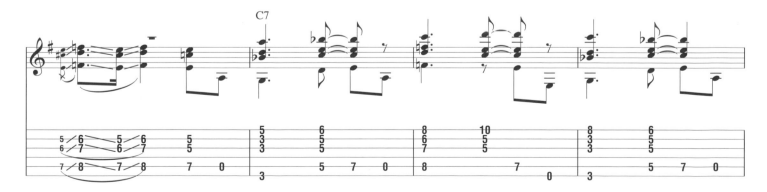

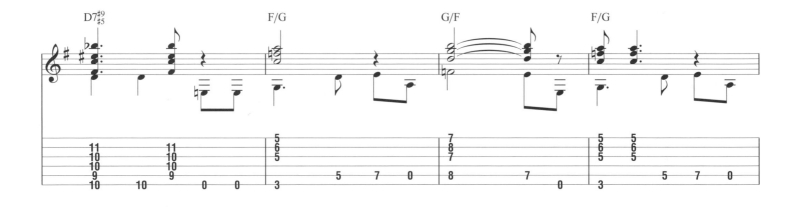

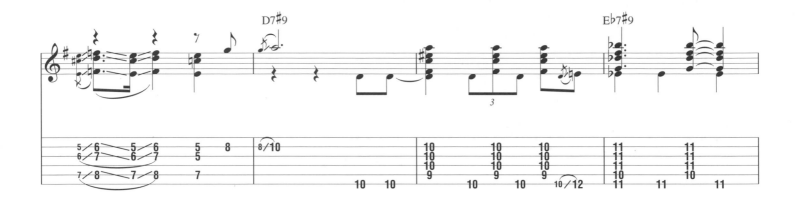

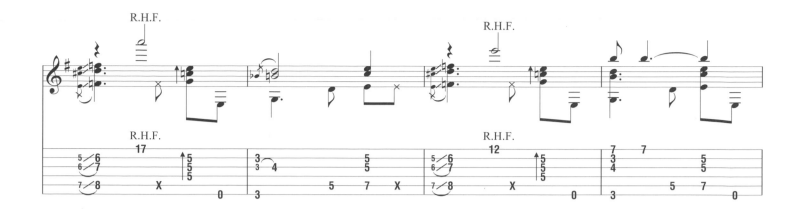

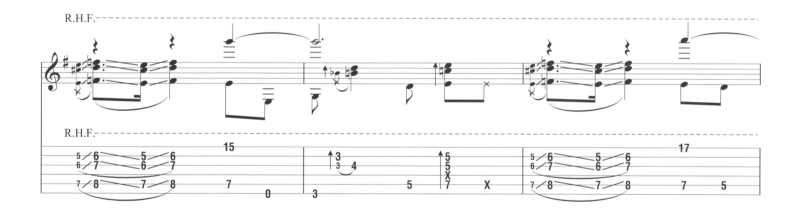

Repeat and fade

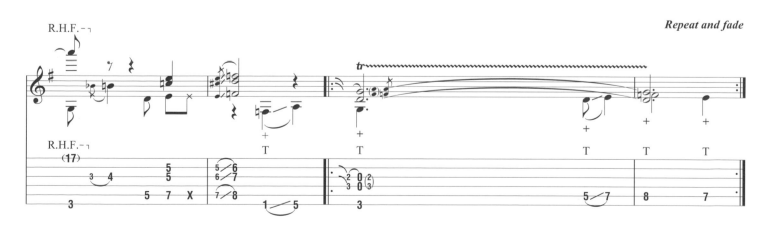

Confirmation

By Charlie Parker

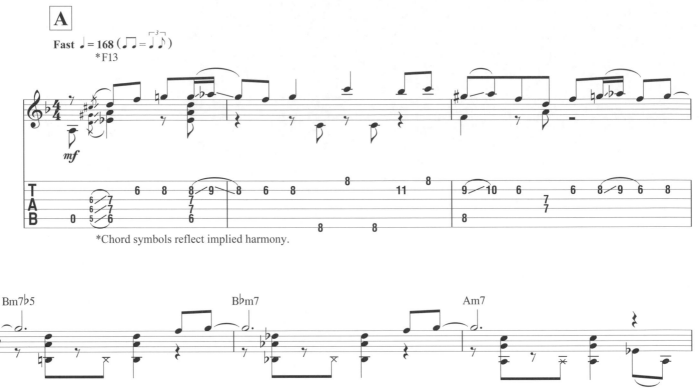

*Chord symbols reflect implied harmony.

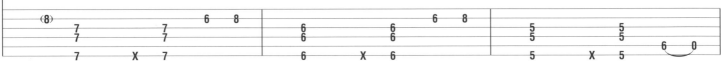

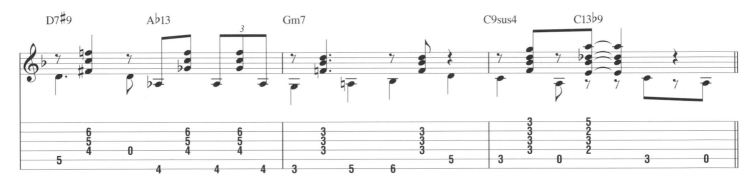

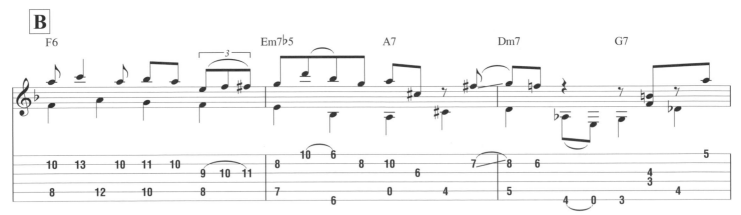

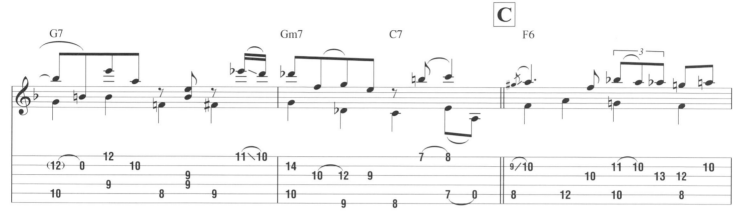

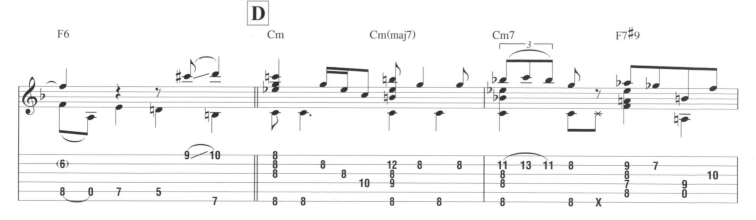

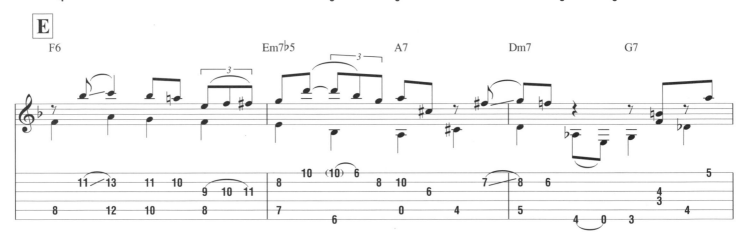

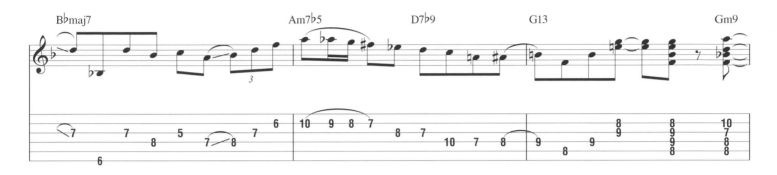

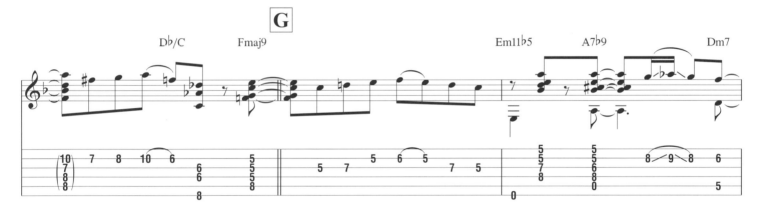

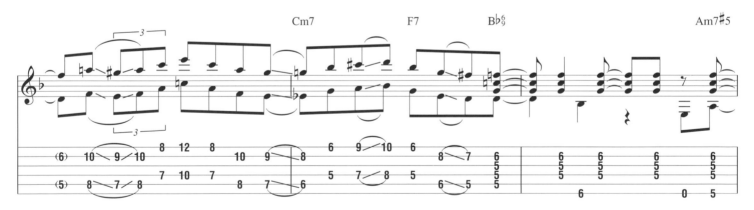

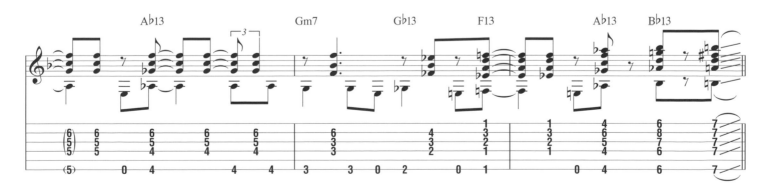

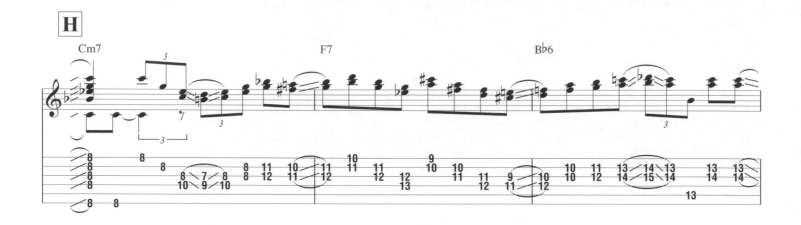

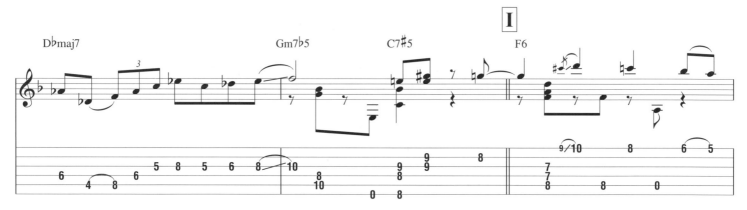

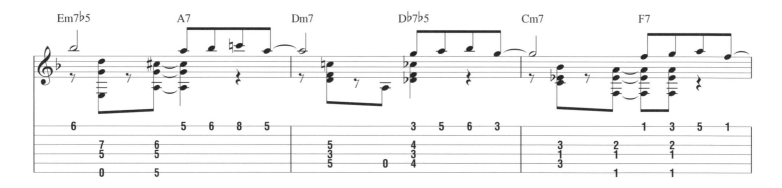

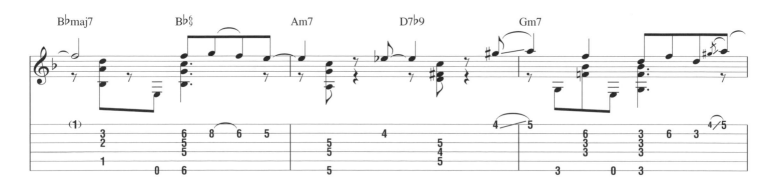

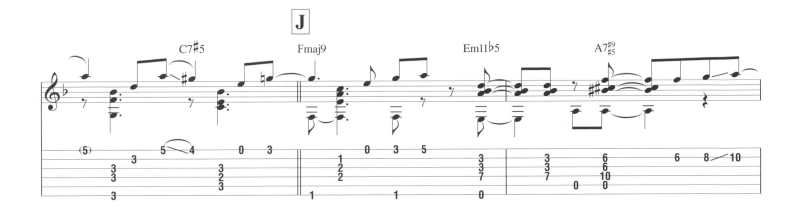

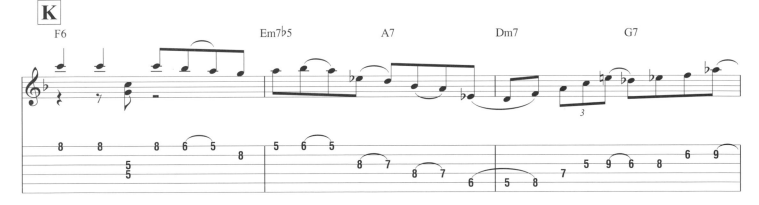

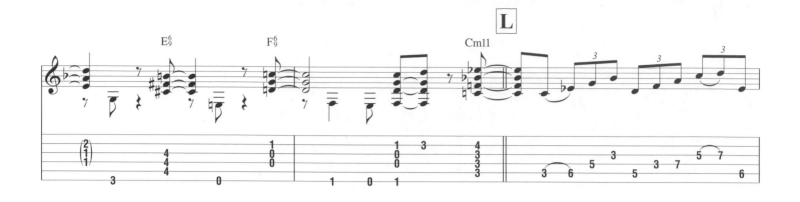

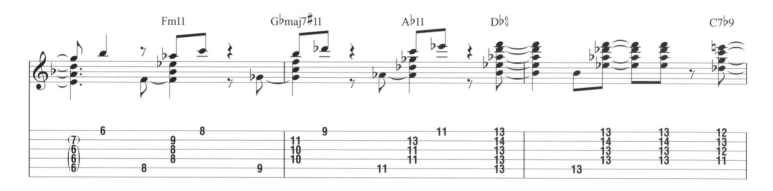

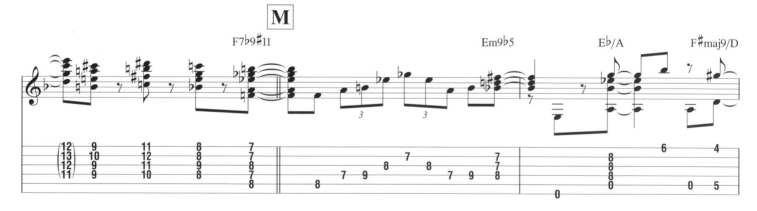

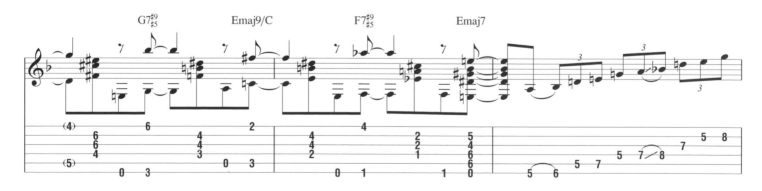

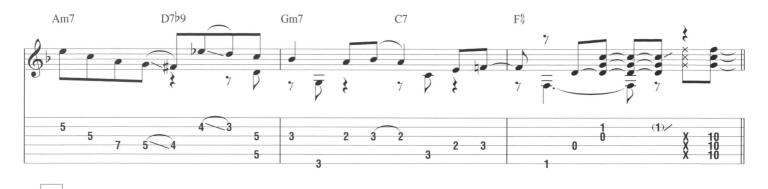

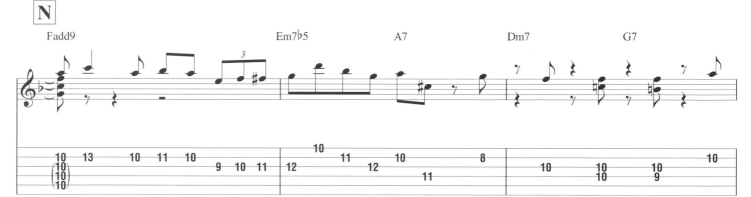

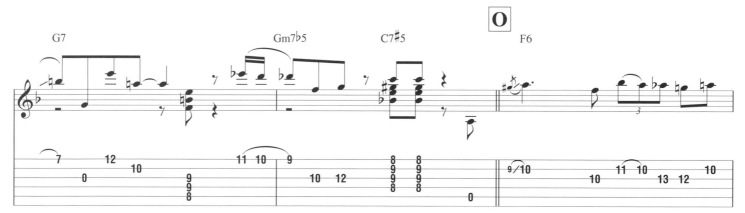

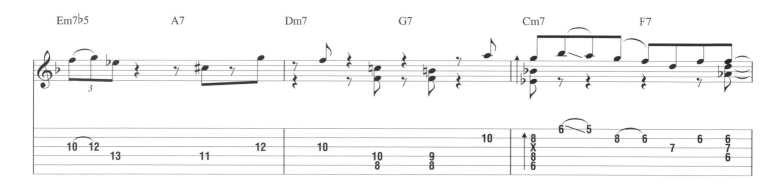

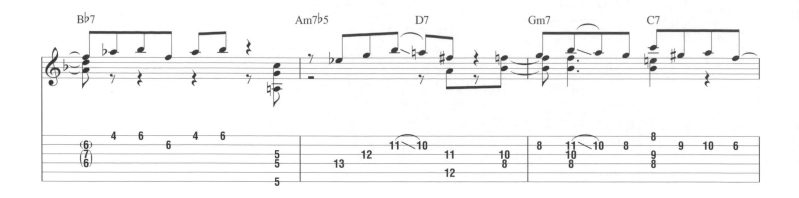

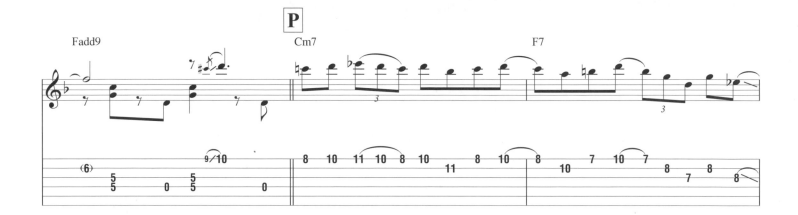

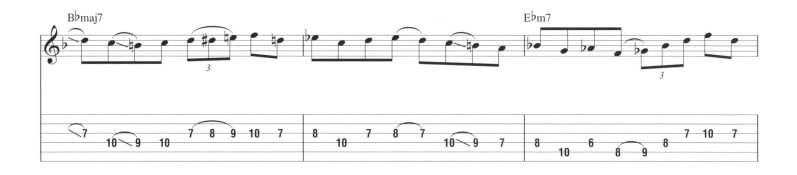

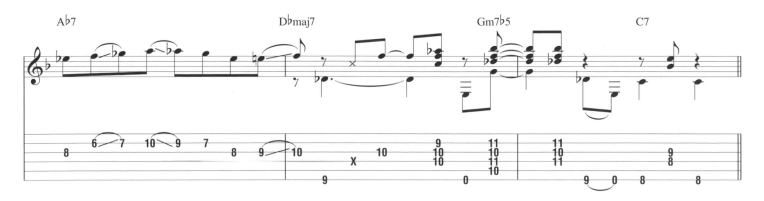

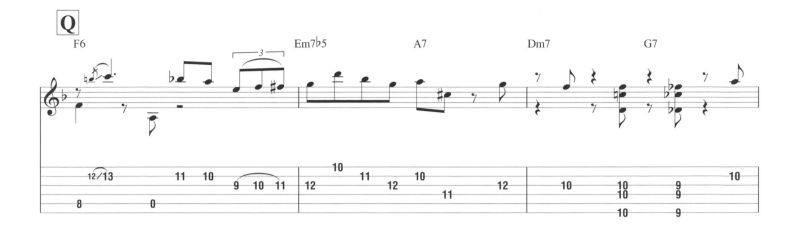

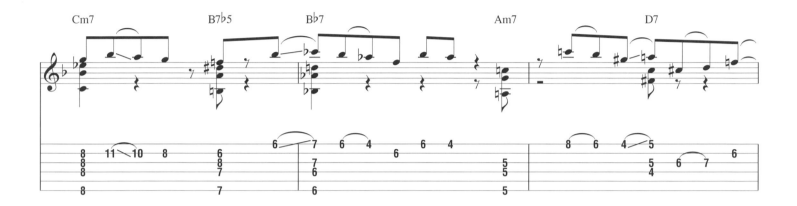

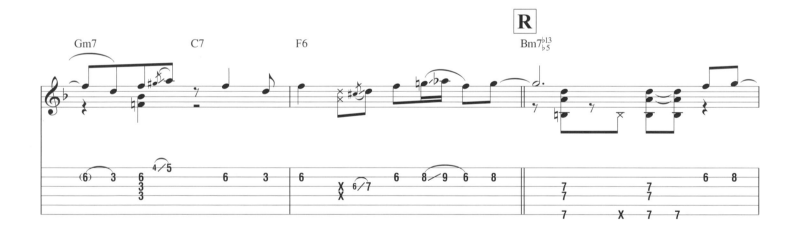

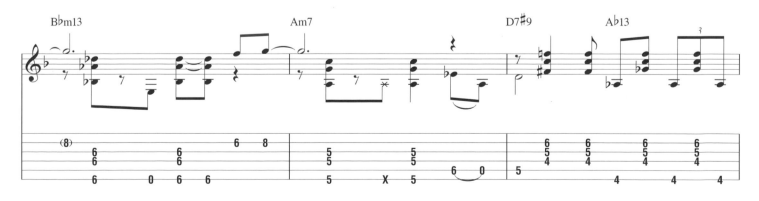

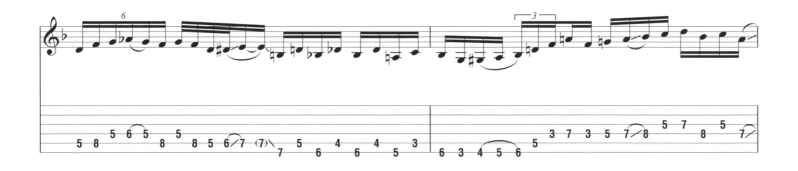

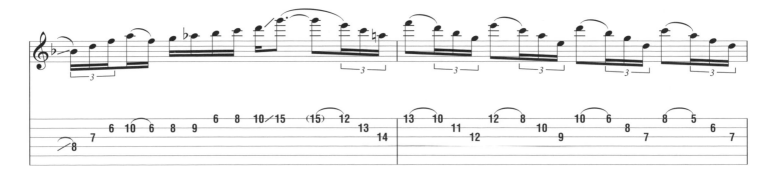

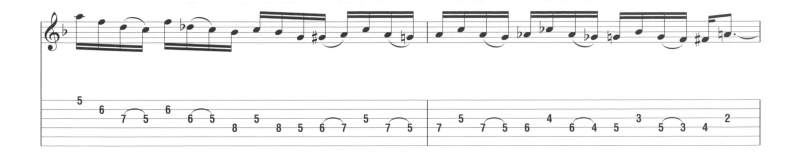

Cadd9/E   N.C.

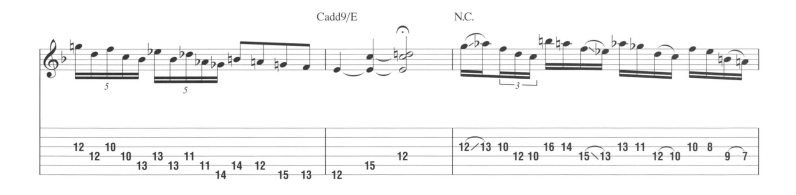

A Tempo
F6♯11

rit.   *let ring* - ⌐   *rit.*

Get Me to the Church on Time

from MY FAIR LADY

Words by Alan Jay Lerner
Music by Frederick Loewe

Drop D tuning:
Low to high: D-A-D-G-B-E

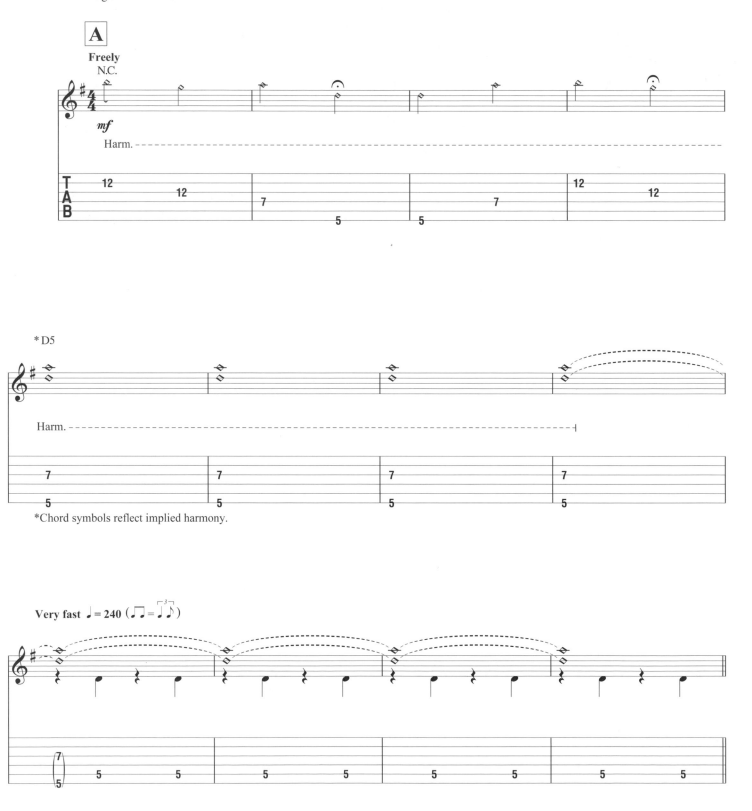

*Chord symbols reflect implied harmony.

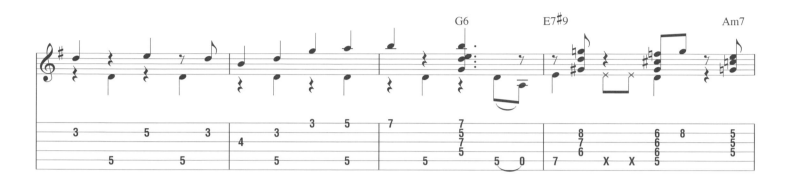

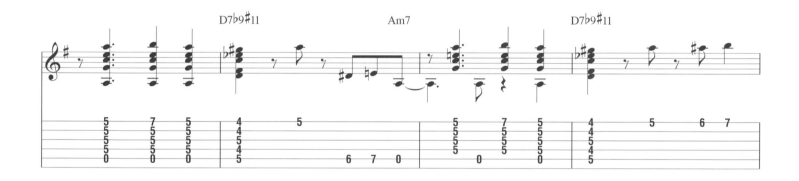

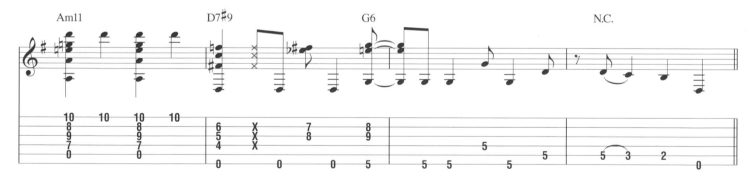

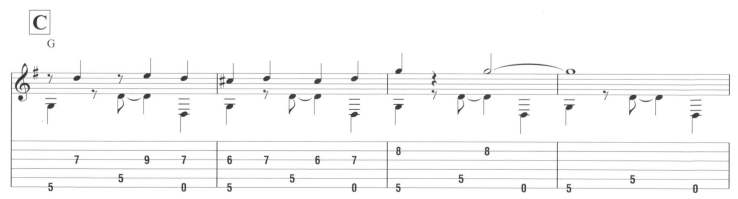

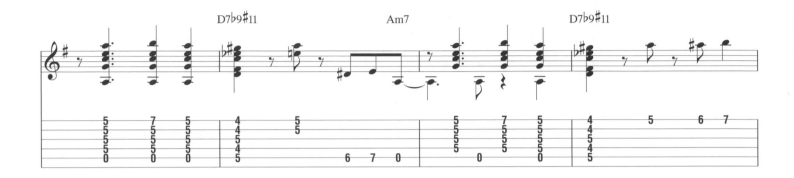

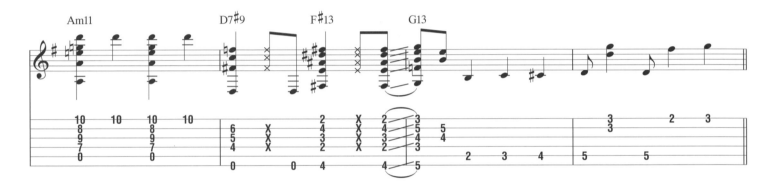

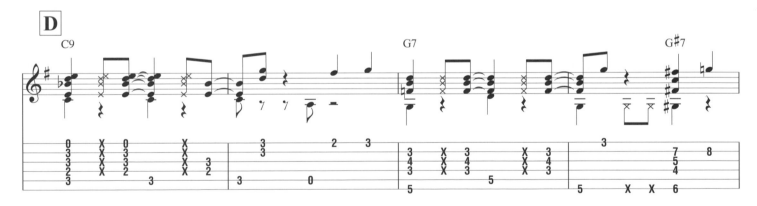

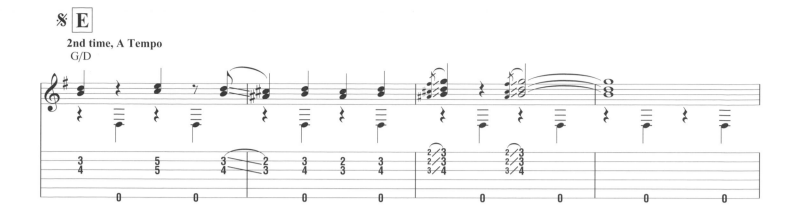

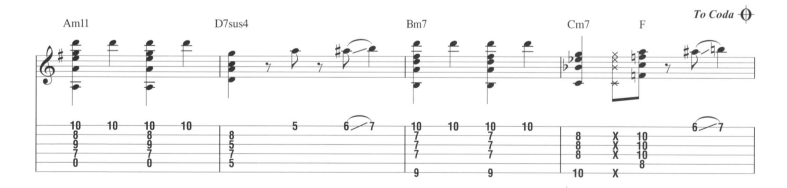

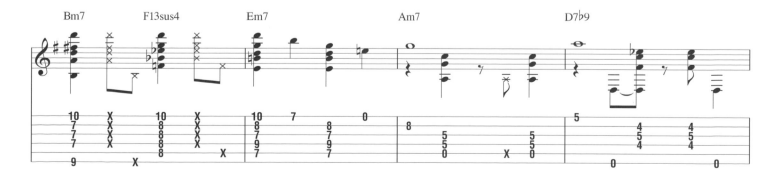

F

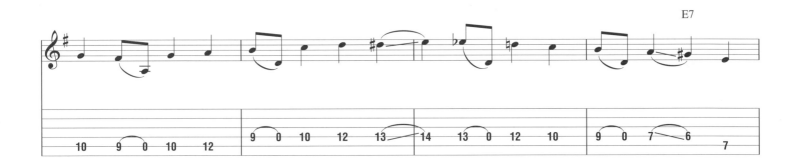

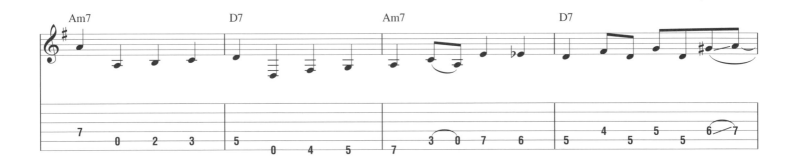

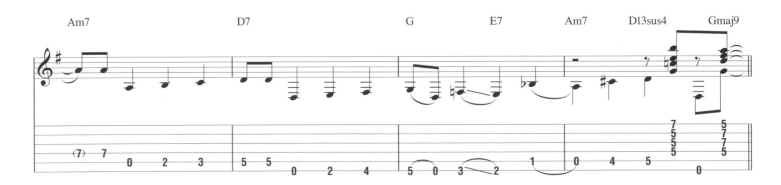

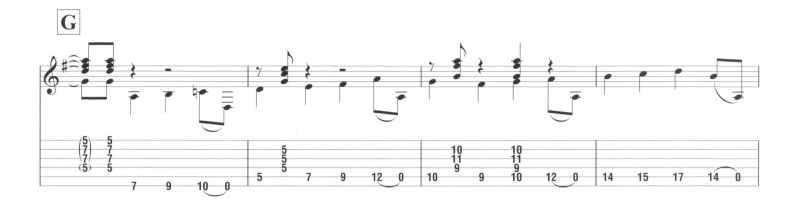

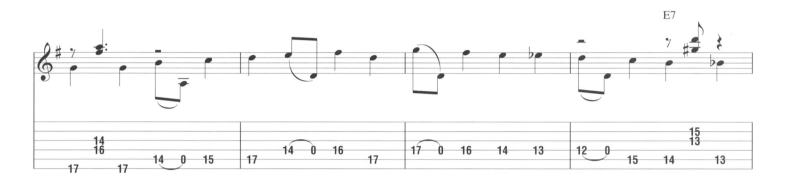

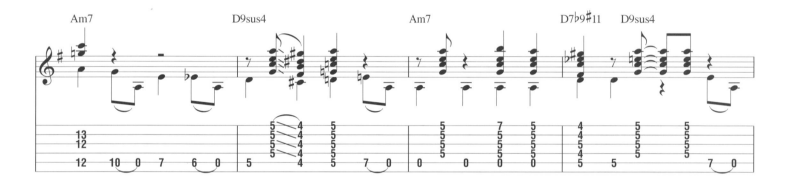

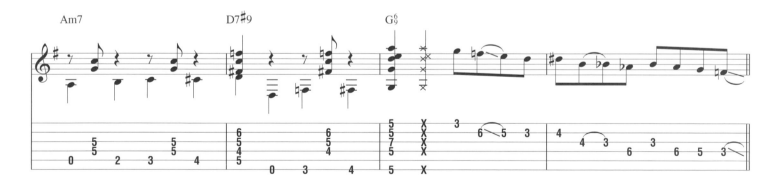

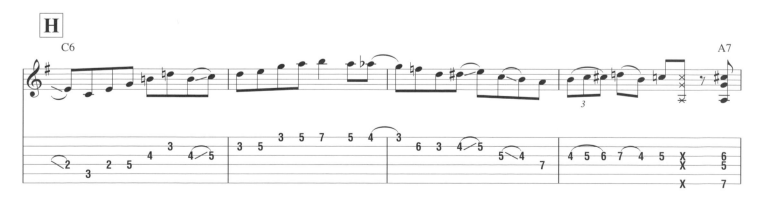

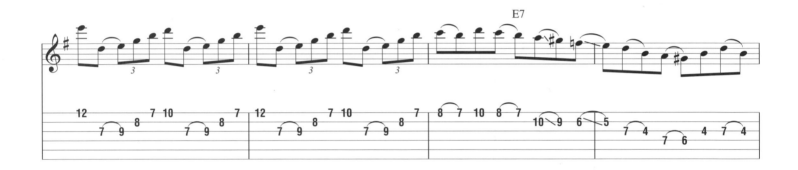

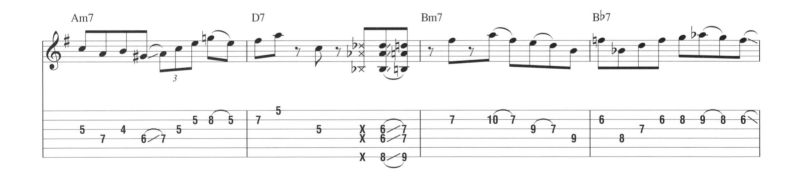

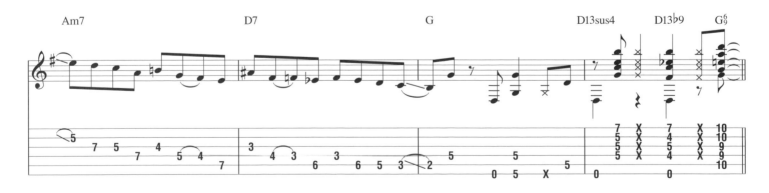

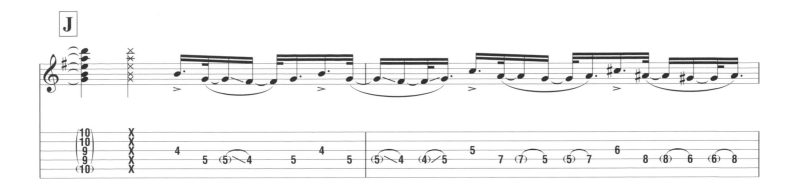

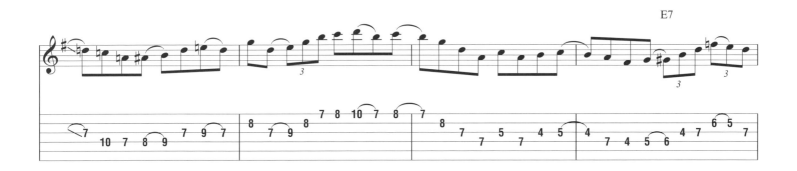

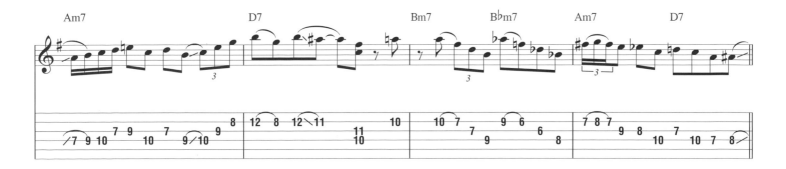

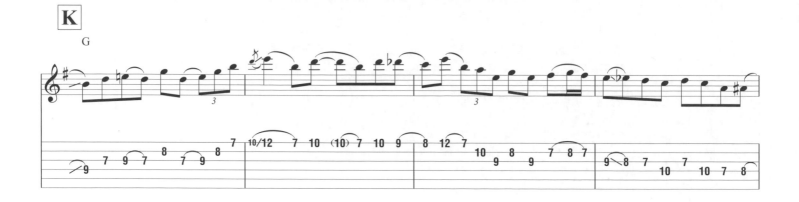

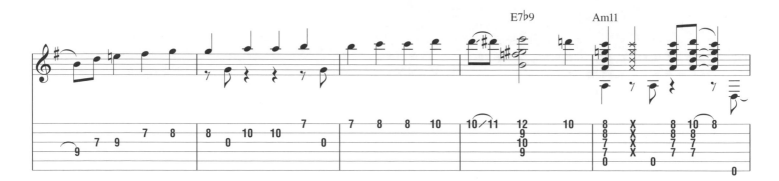

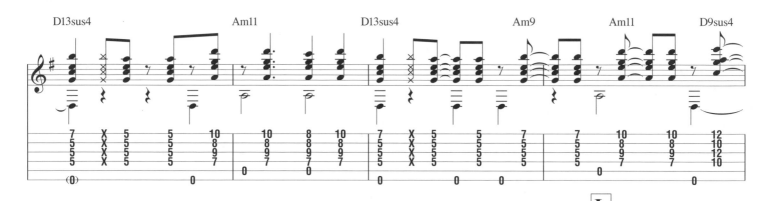

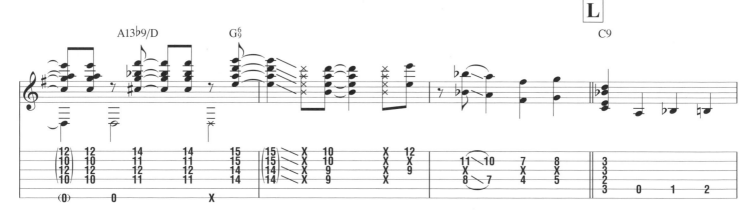

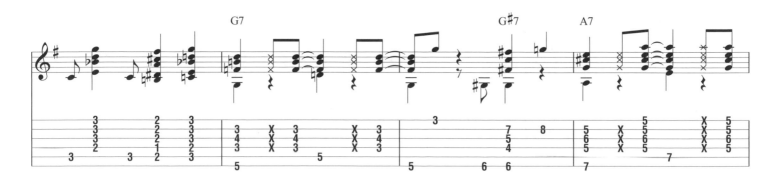

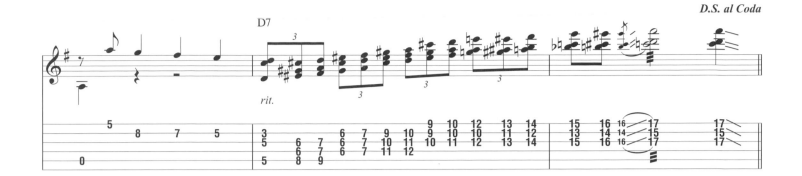

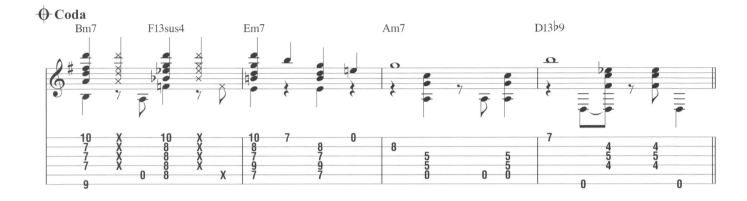

Coda

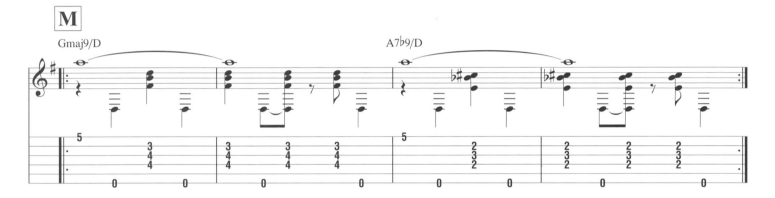

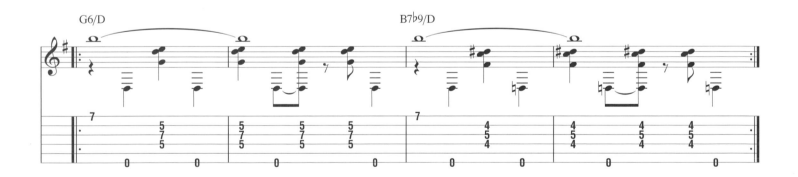

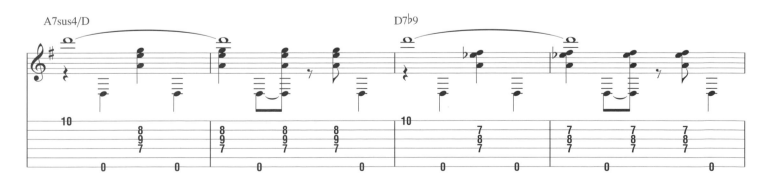

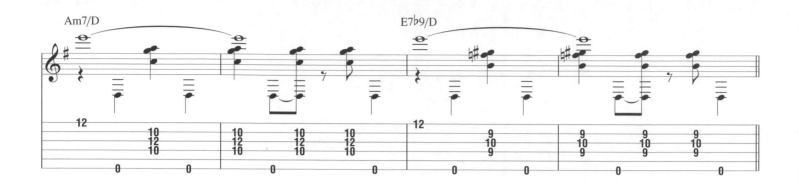

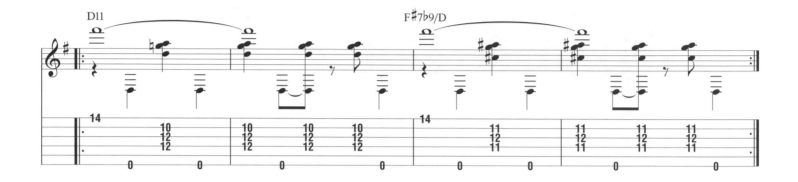

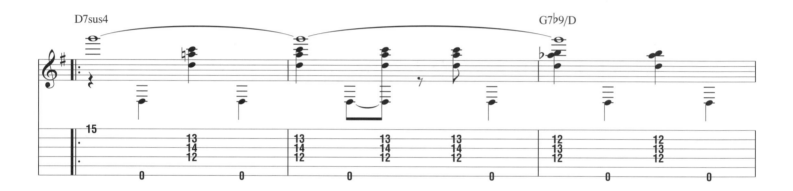

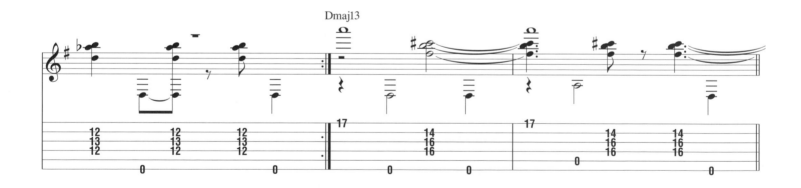

I'm Old Fashioned

from YOU WERE NEVER LOVELIER

Lyrics by Johnny Mercer
Music by Jerome Kern

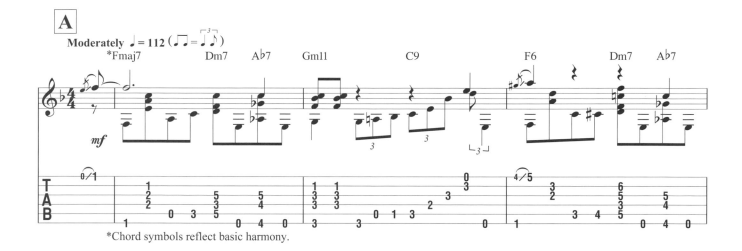

*Chord symbols reflect basic harmony.

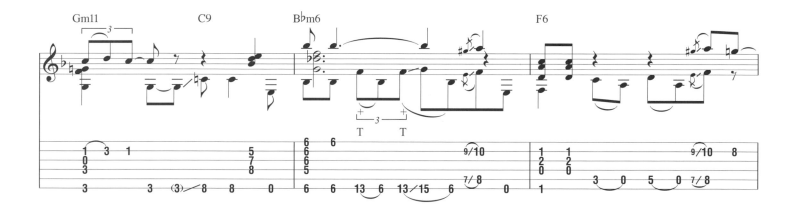

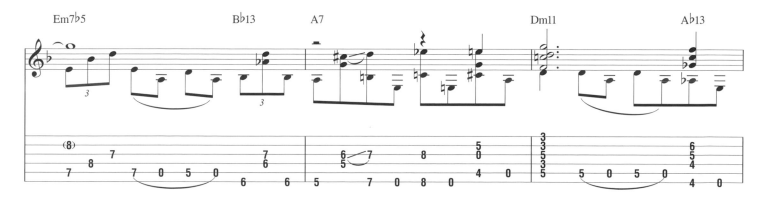

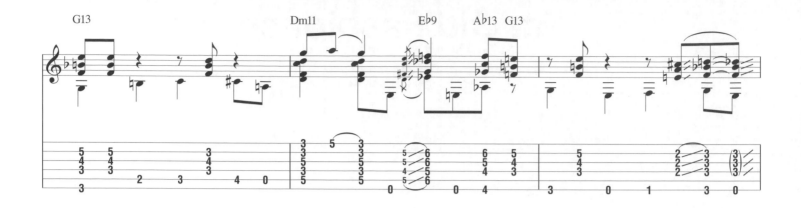

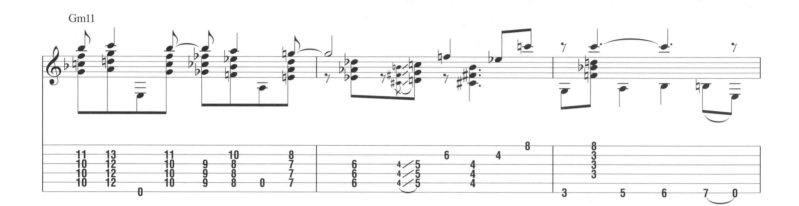

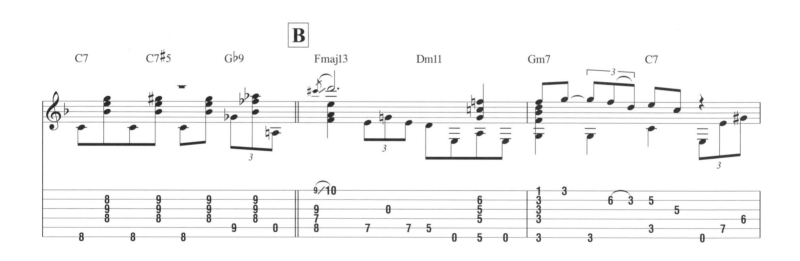

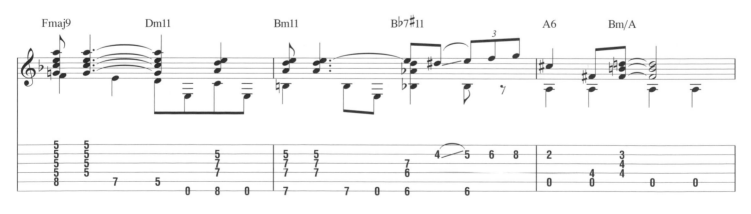

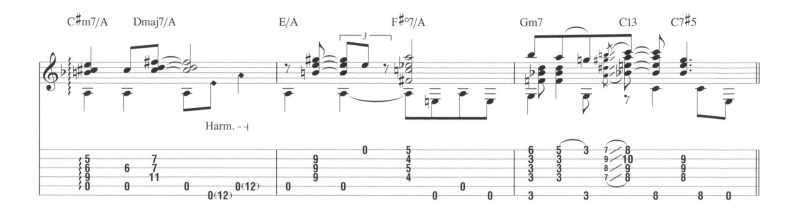

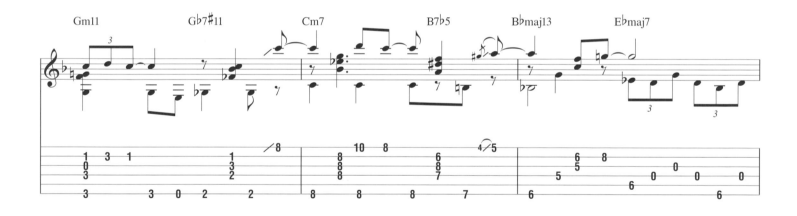

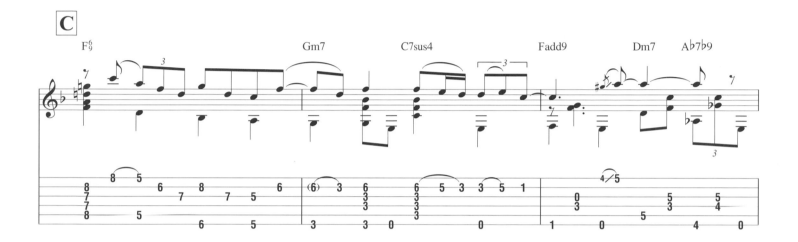

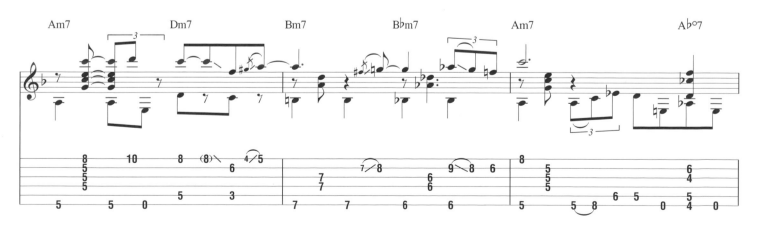

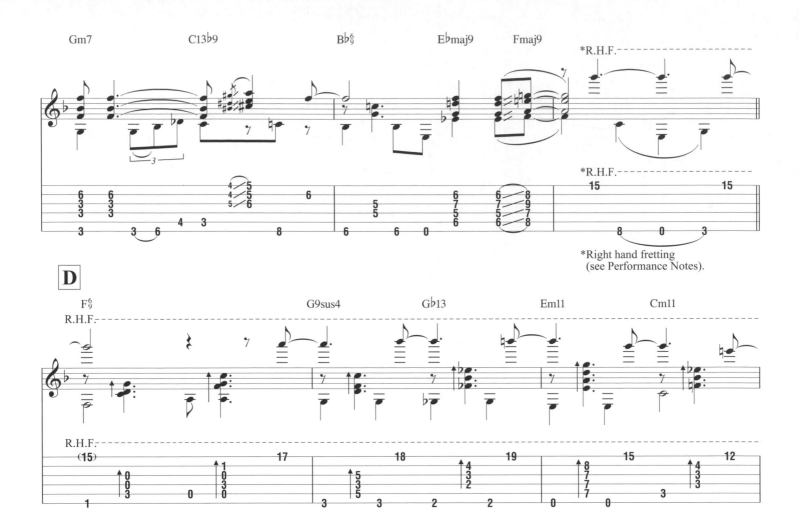

*Right hand fretting
(see Performance Notes).

D

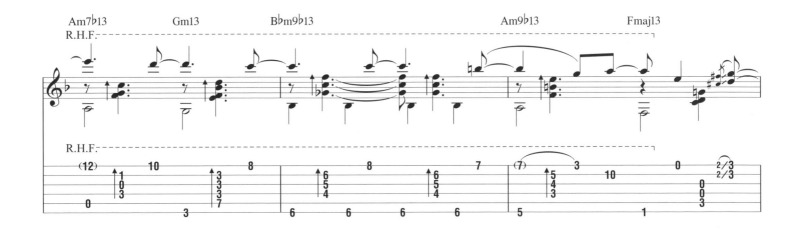

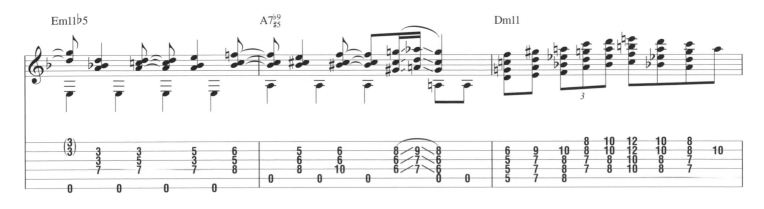

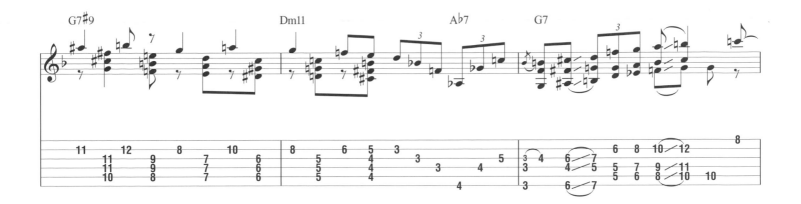

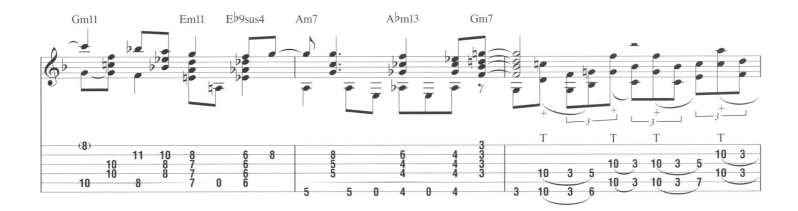

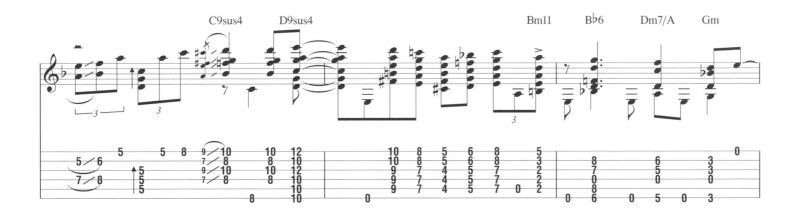

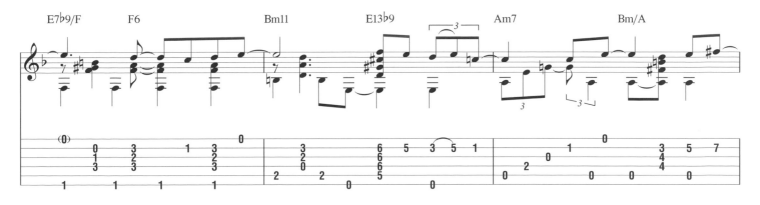

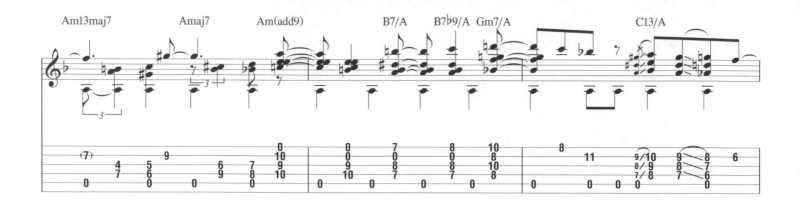

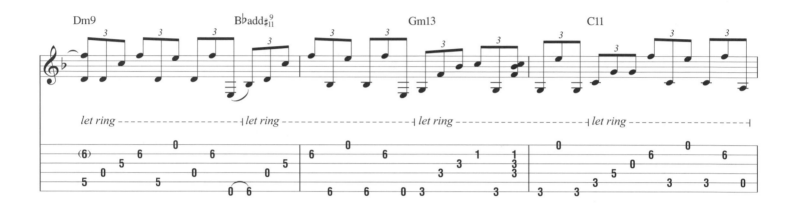

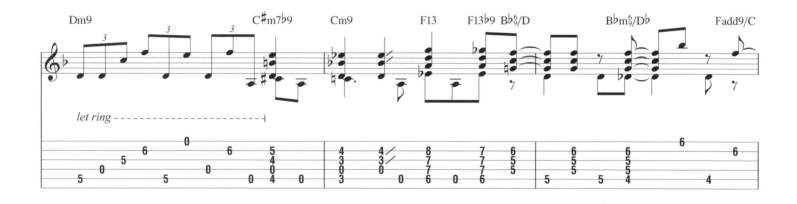

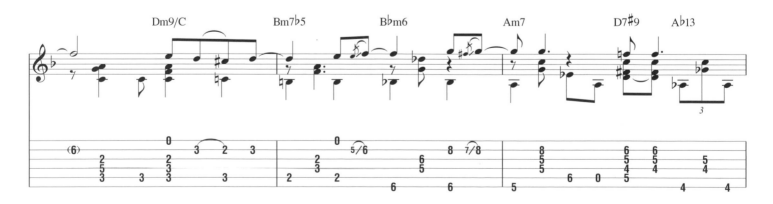

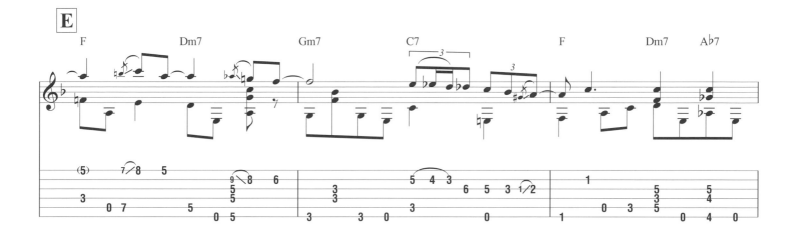

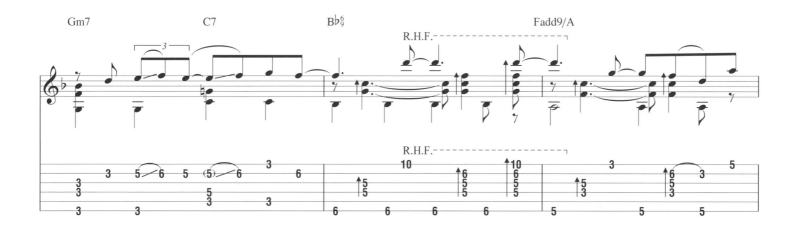

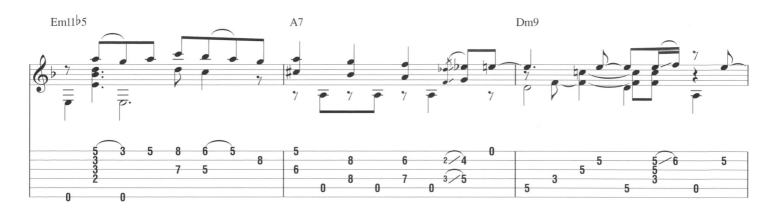

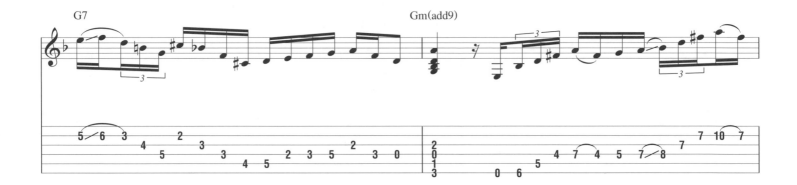

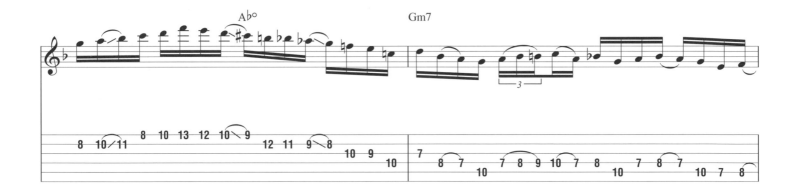

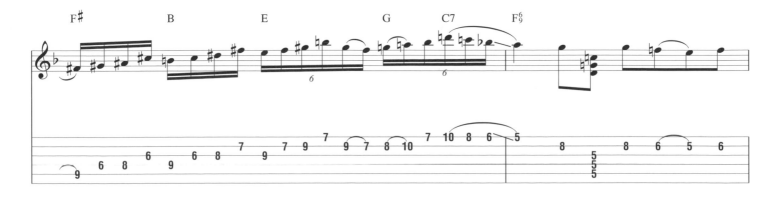

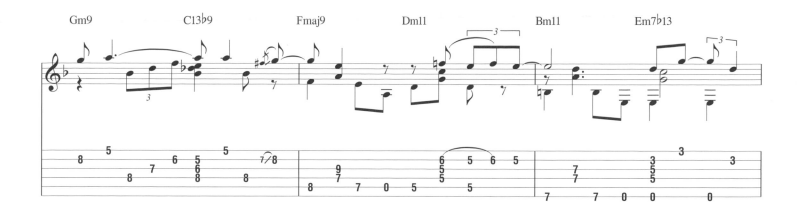

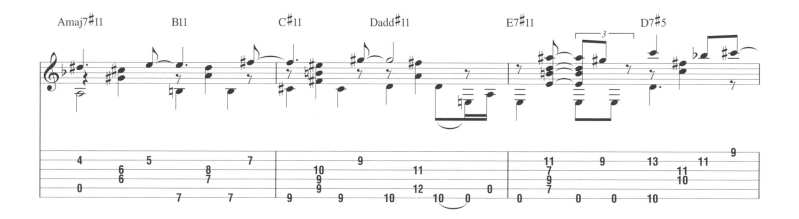

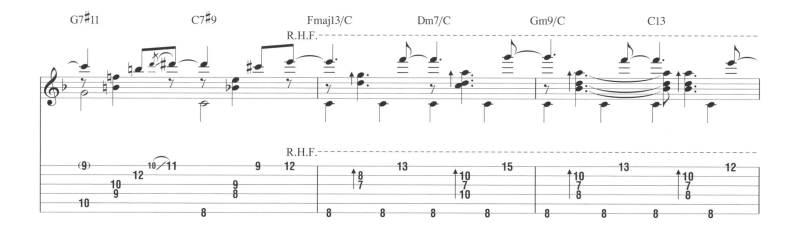

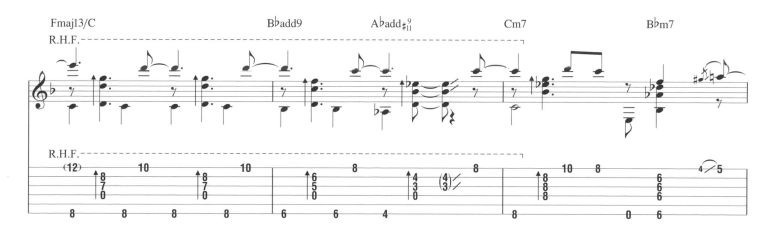

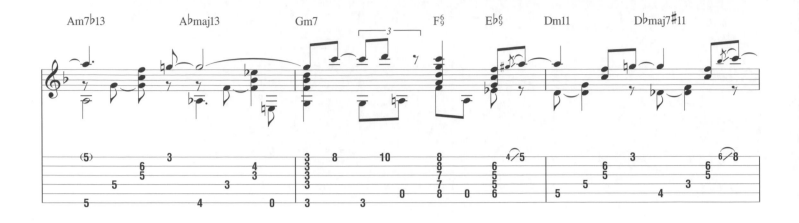

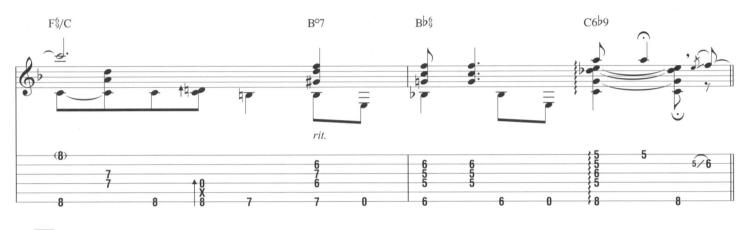

A Tempo

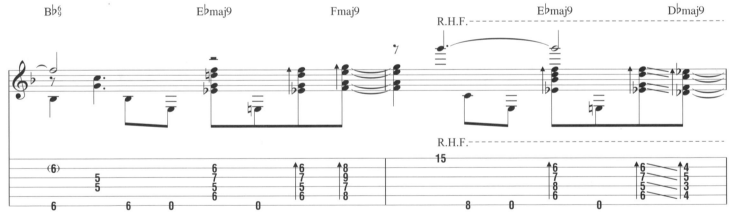

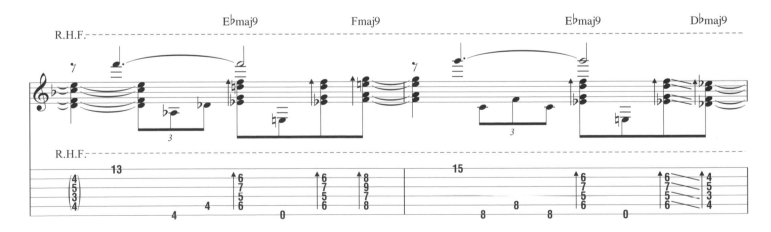

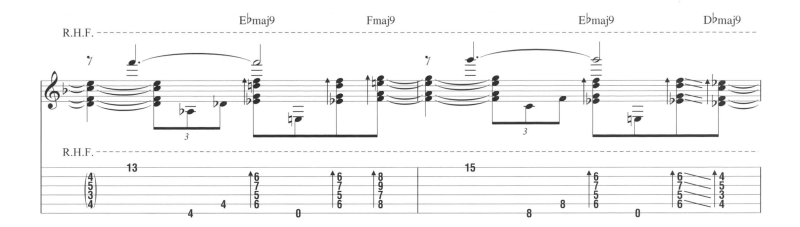

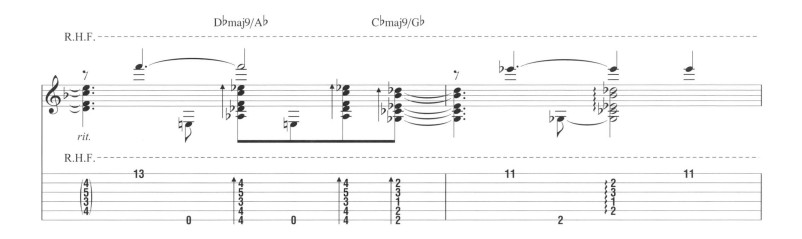

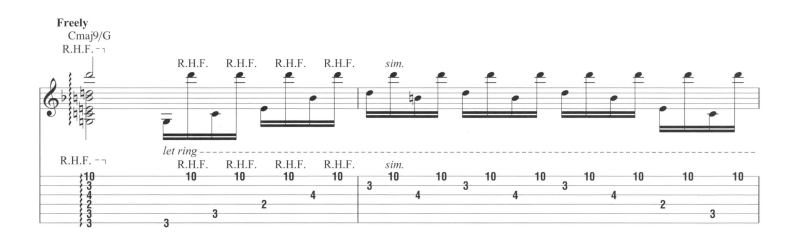

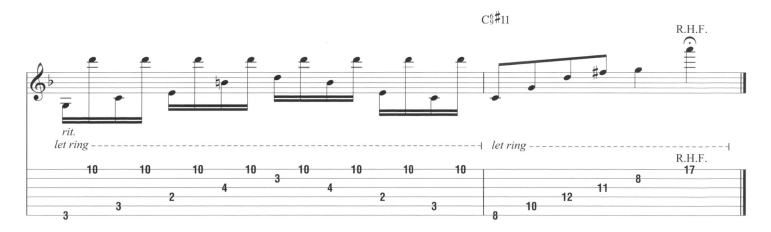

My Romance

from JUMBO

Words by Lorenz Hart
Music by Richard Rodgers

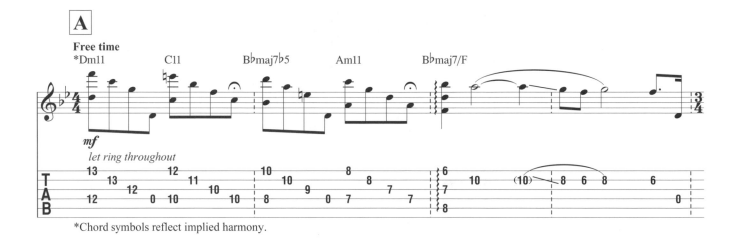

*Chord symbols reflect implied harmony.

*Right hand fretting (see Performance Notes),
1st & 5th strings only.

**Next 38 meas.

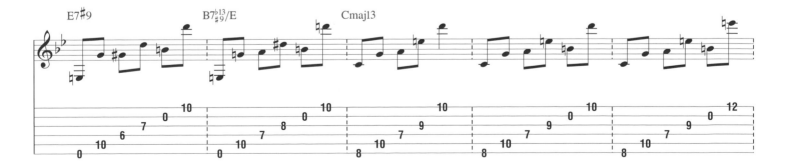

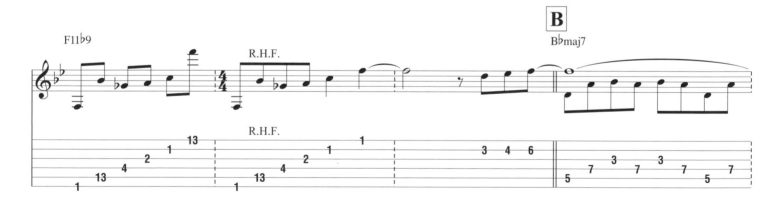

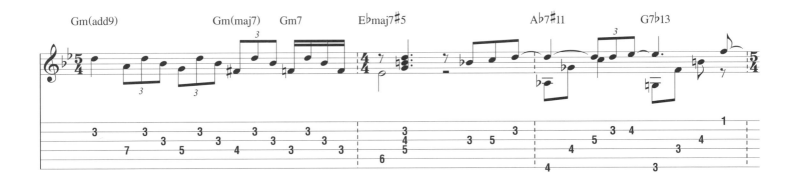

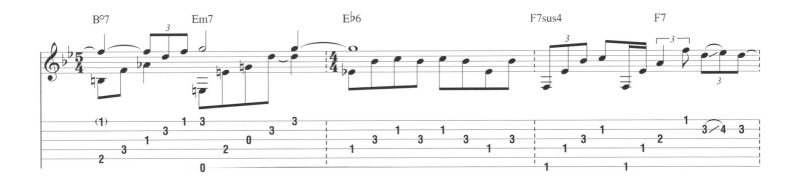

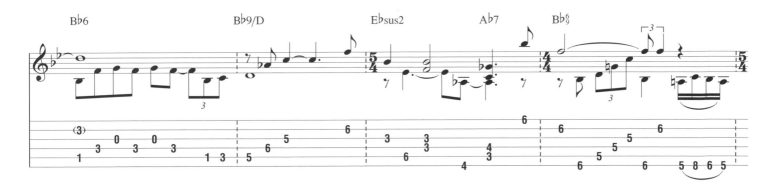

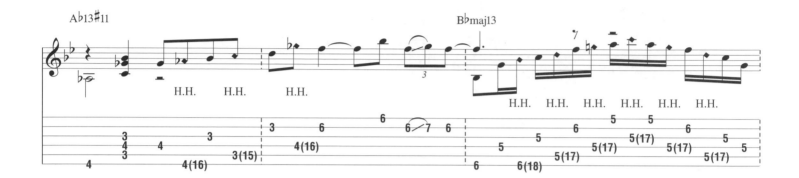

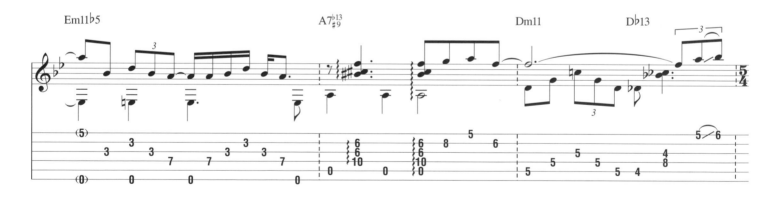

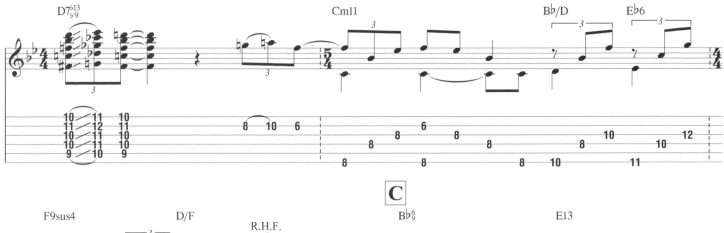

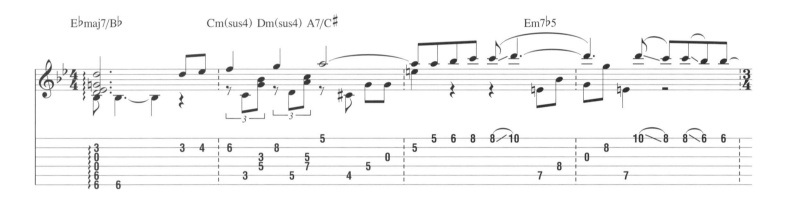

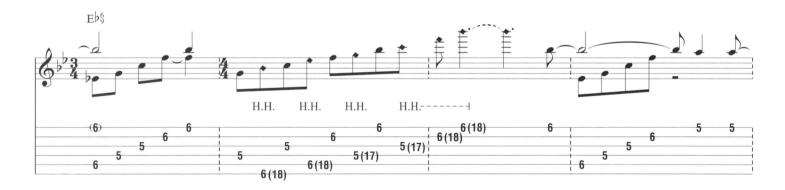

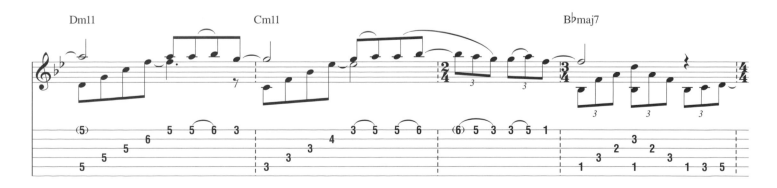

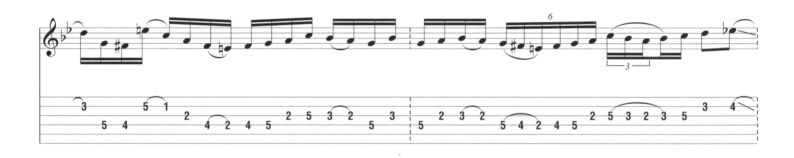

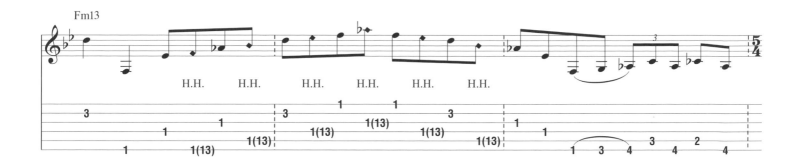

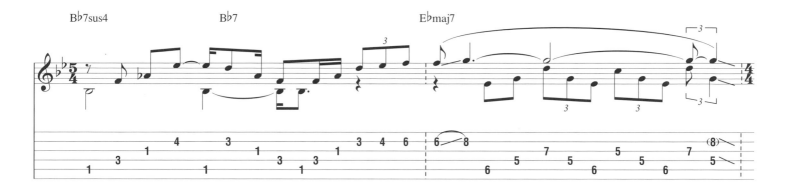

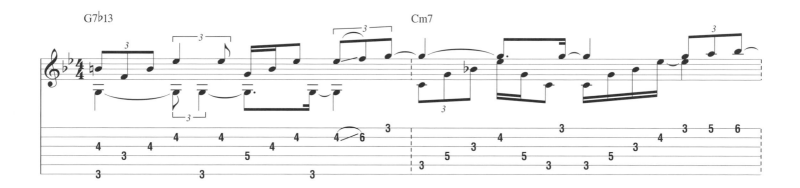

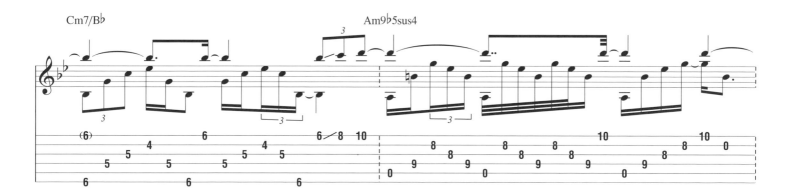

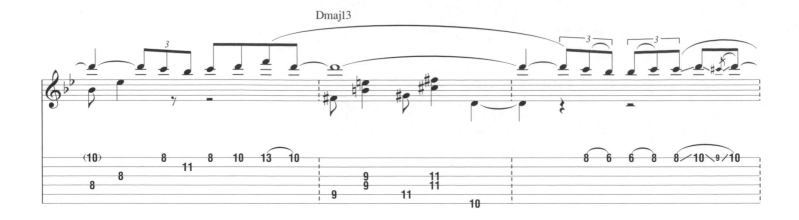

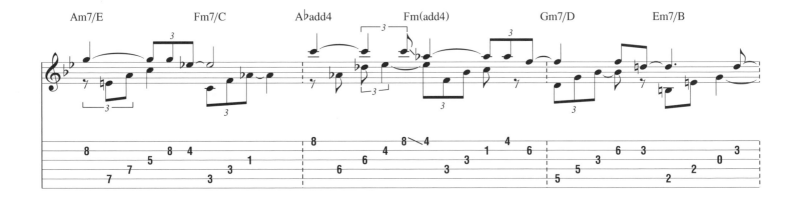

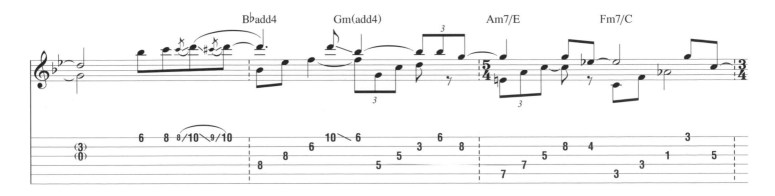

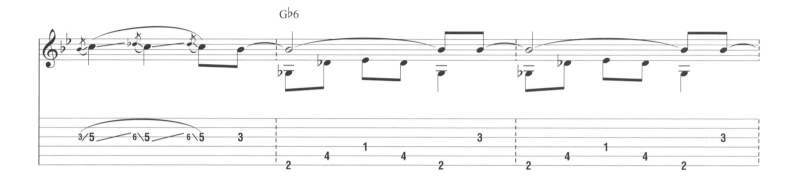

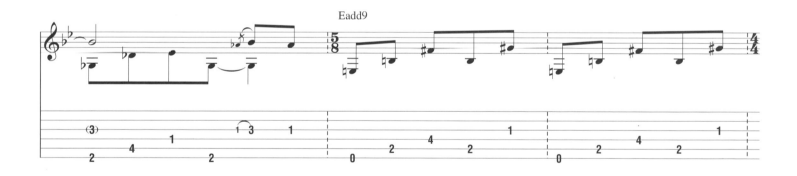

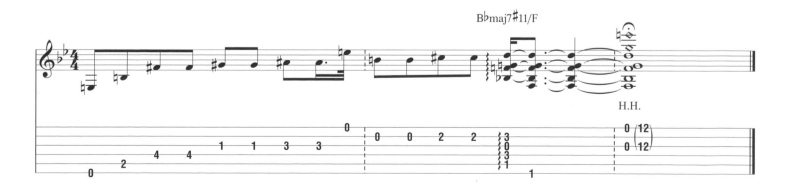

On the Street Where You Live

from MY FAIR LADY

Words by Alan Jay Lerner
Music by Frederick Loewe

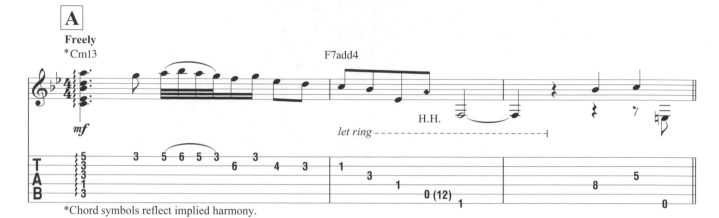

*Chord symbols reflect implied harmony.

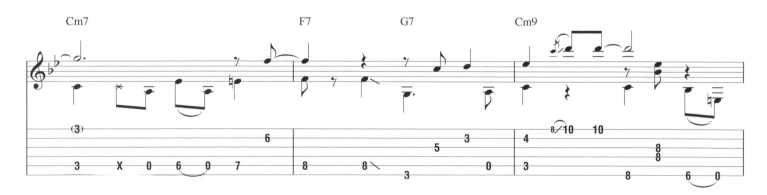

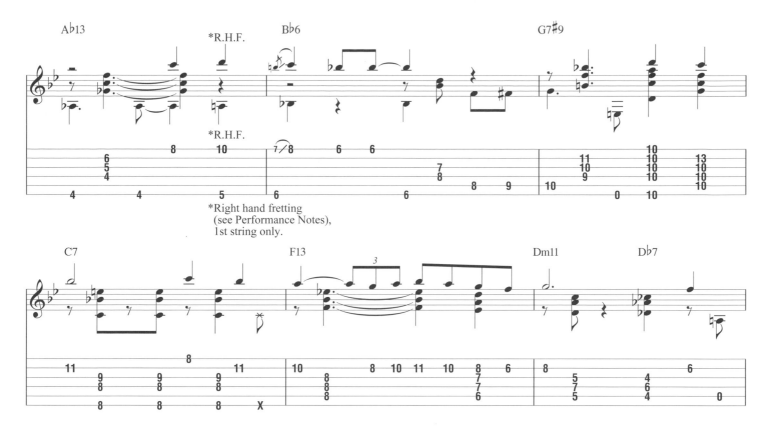

*Right hand fretting
(see Performance Notes),
1st string only.

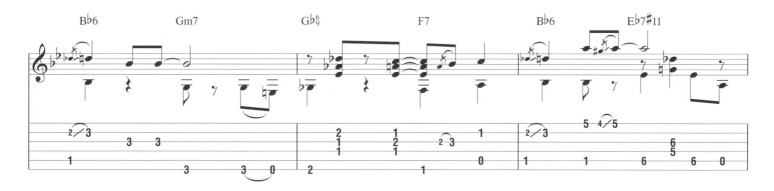

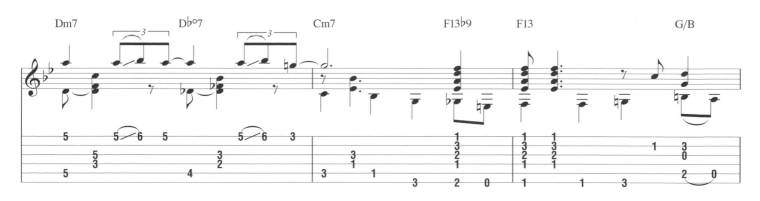

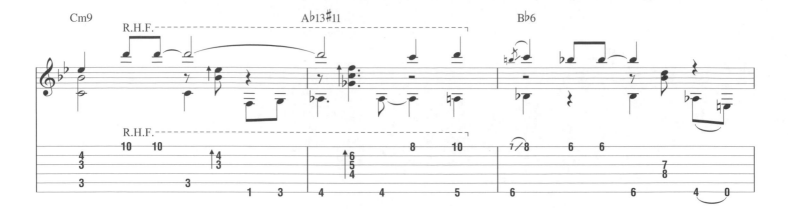

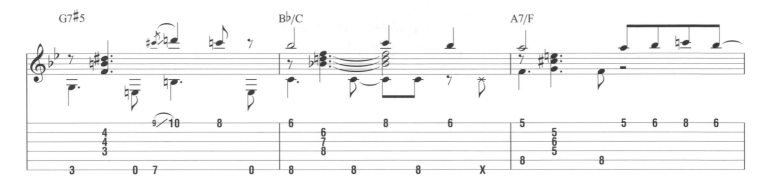

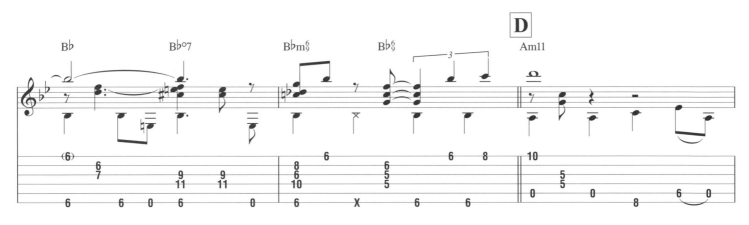

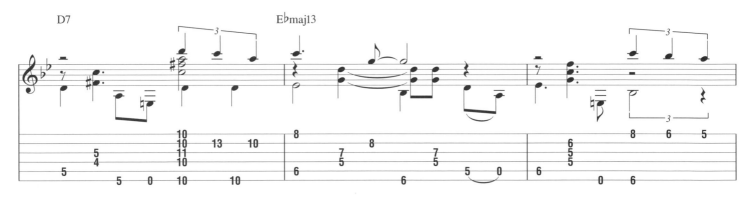

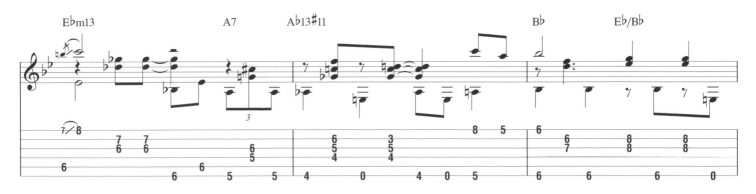

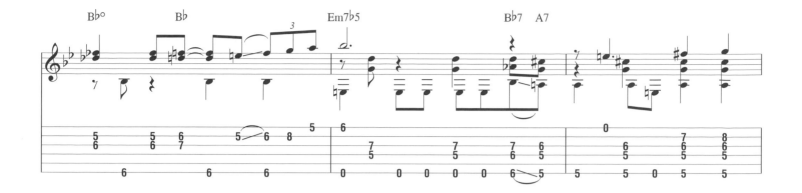

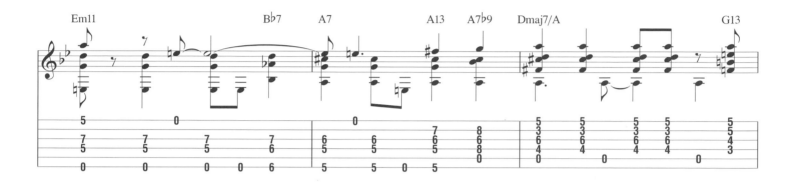

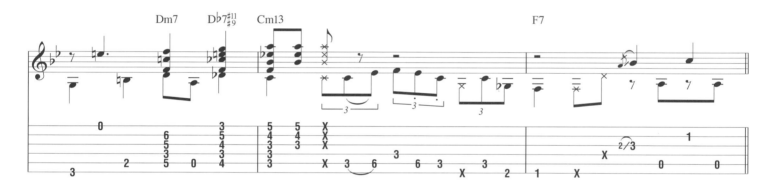

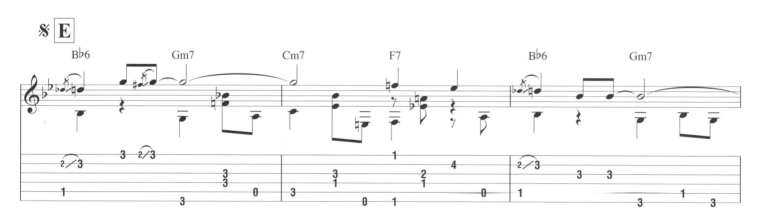

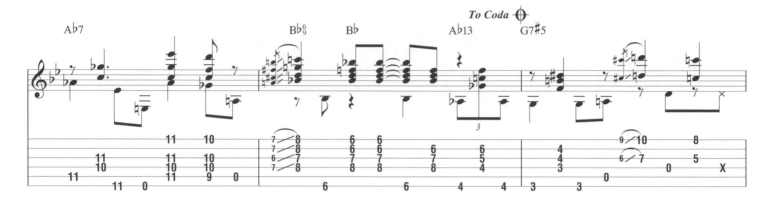

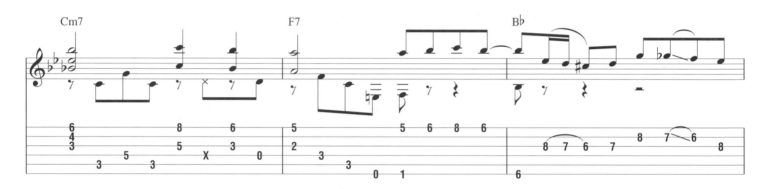

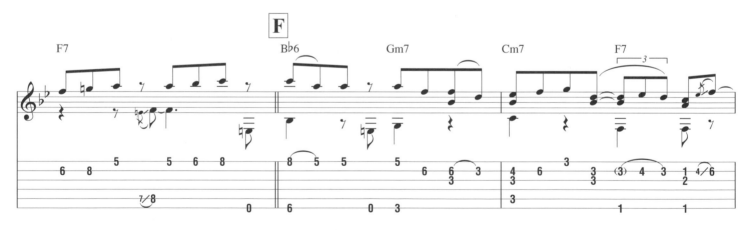

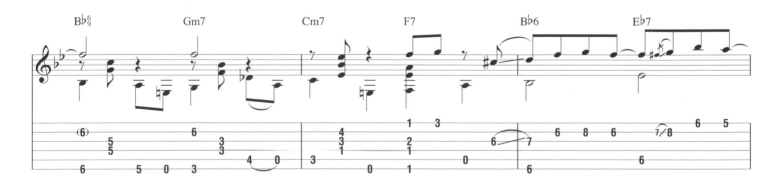

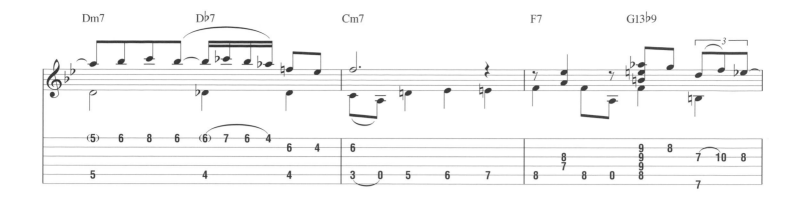

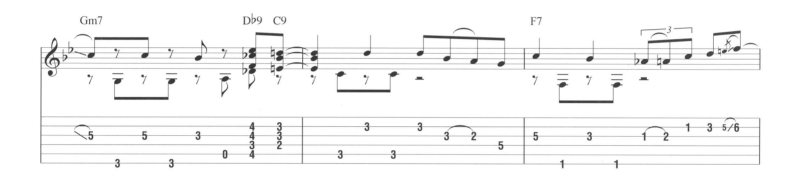

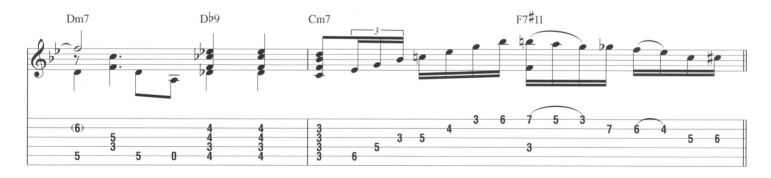

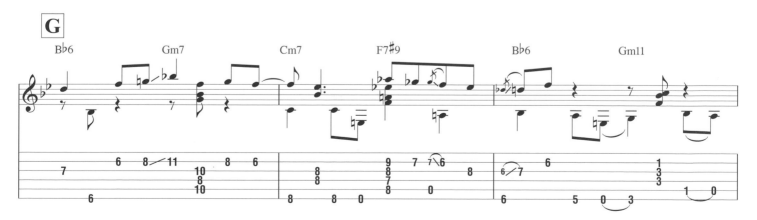

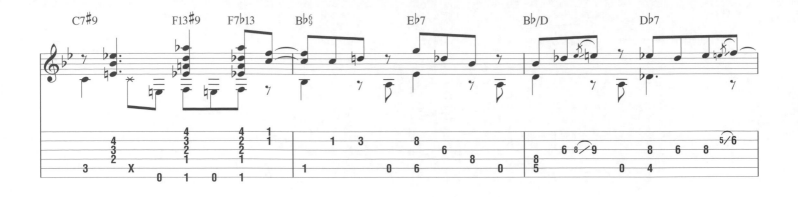

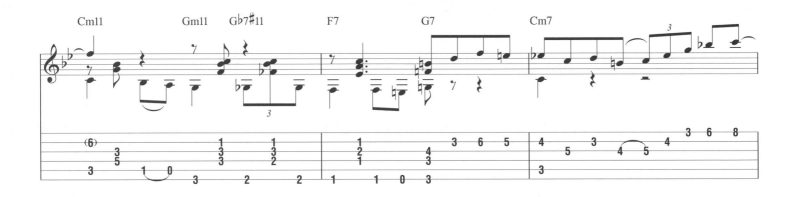

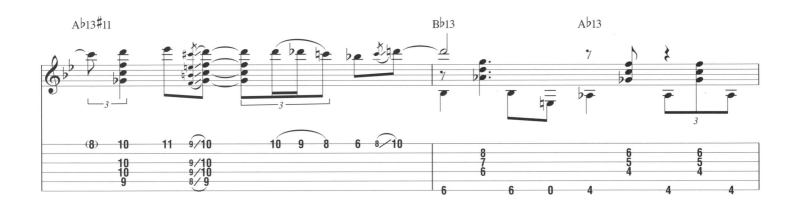

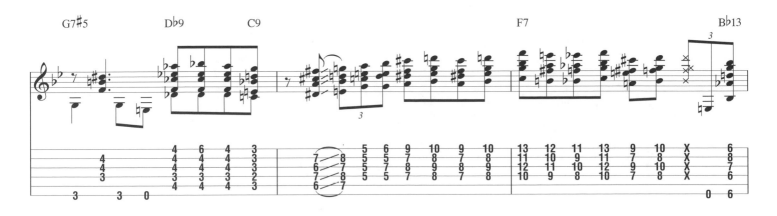

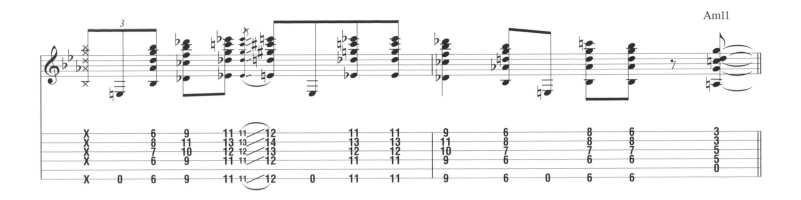

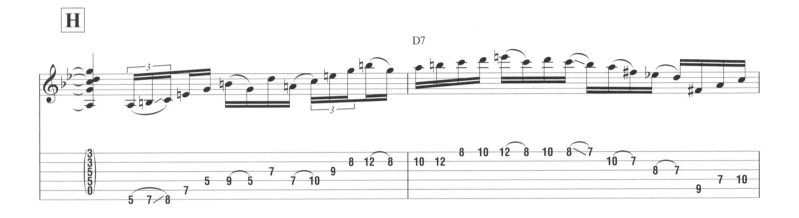

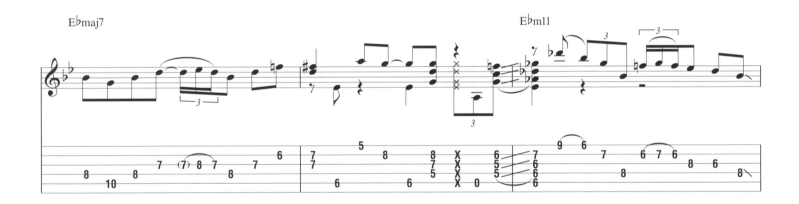

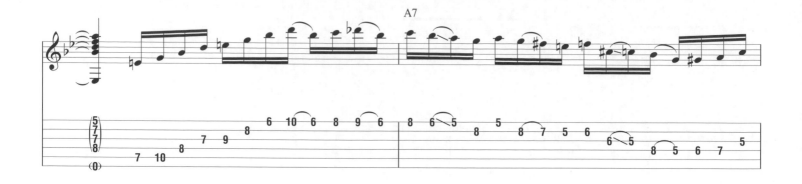

A7

Em7♭5   A7

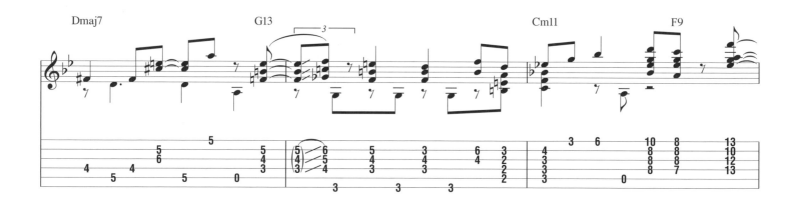

Dmaj7   G13   3   Cm11   F9

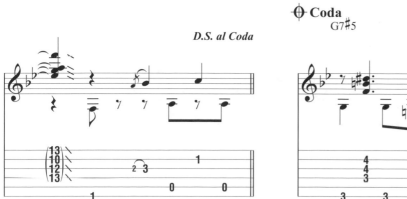

𝄌 **Coda**
G7♯5   Cm7

D.S. al Coda

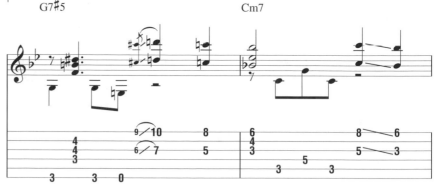

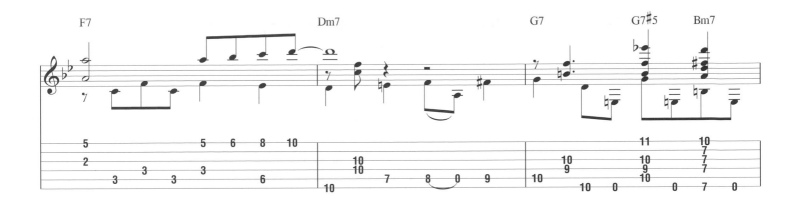

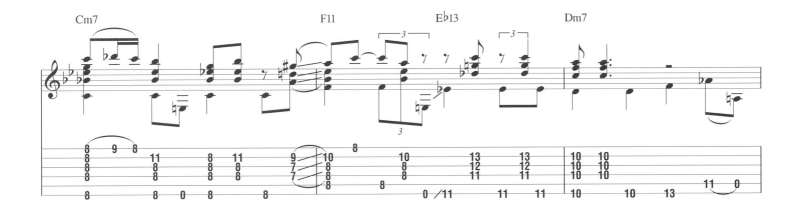

Polka Dots and Moonbeams

Words by Johnny Burke
Music by Jimmy Van Heusen

*Right hand fretting (see Performance Notes).

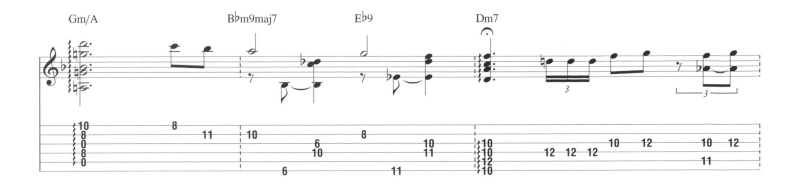

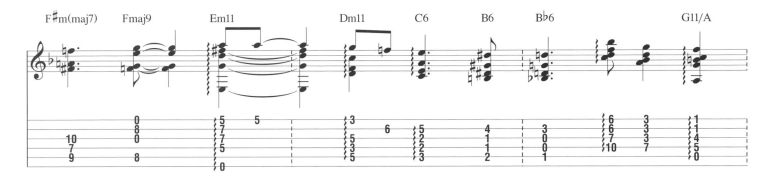

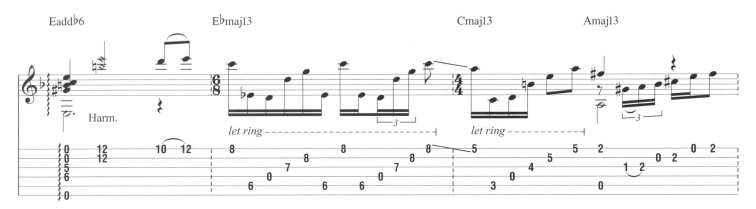

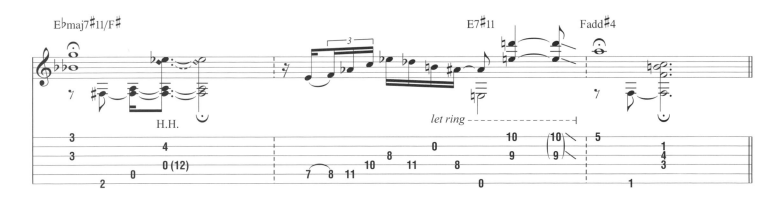

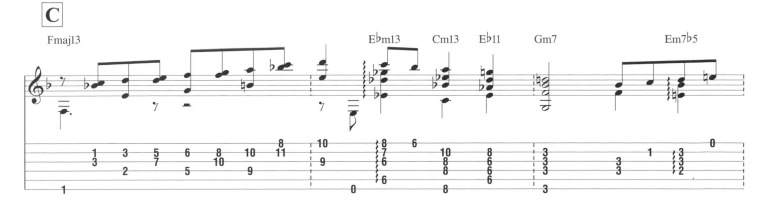

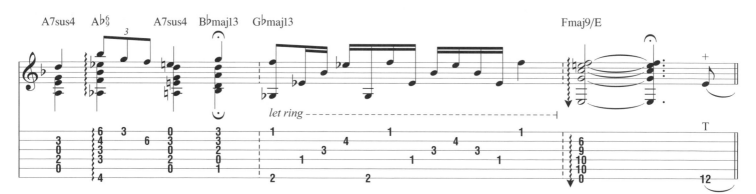

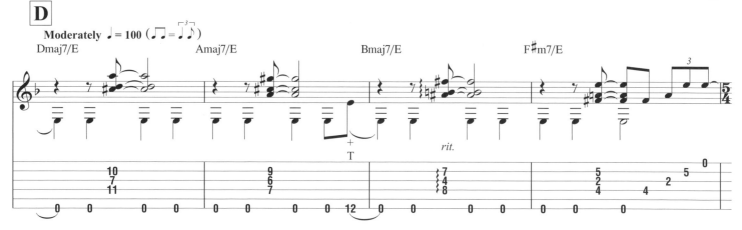

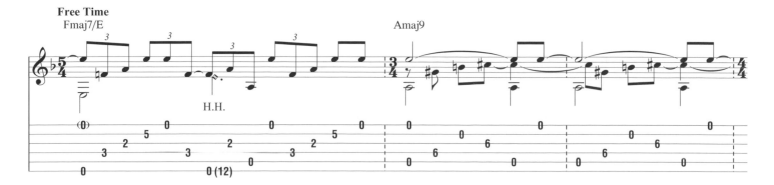

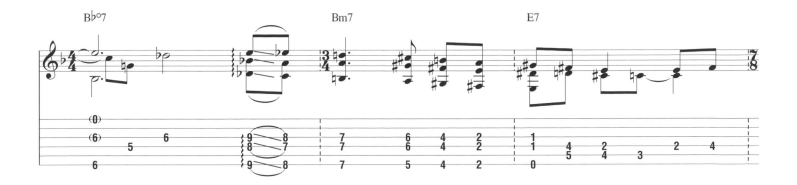

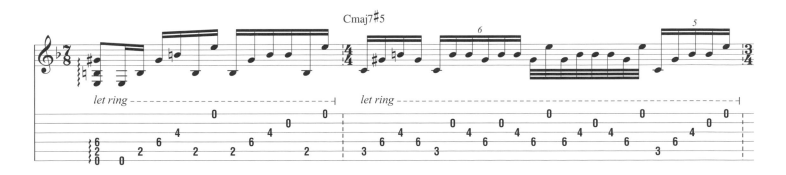

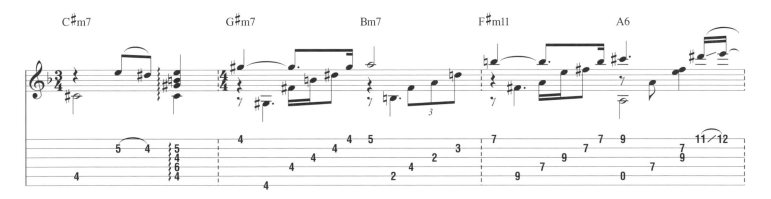

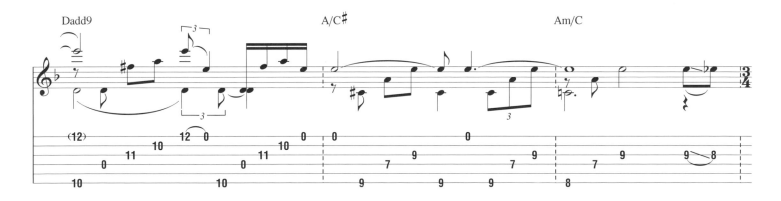

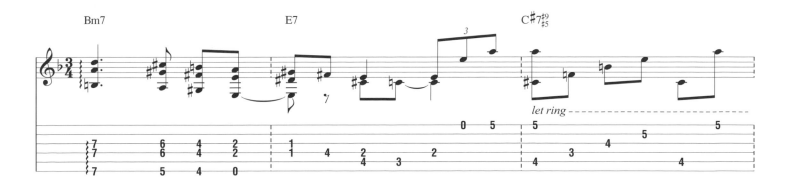

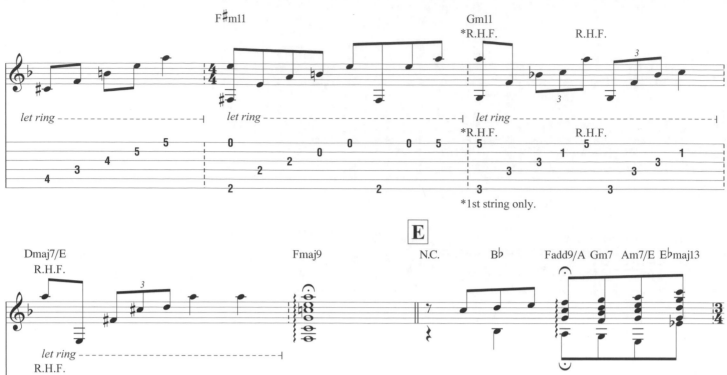

*1st string only.

E

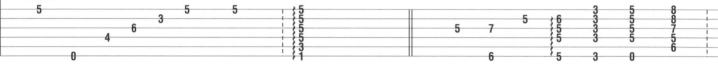

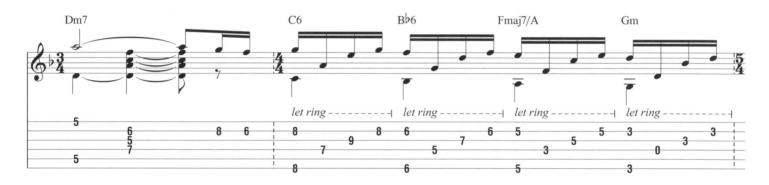

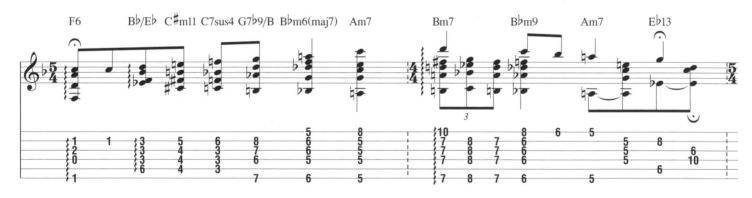

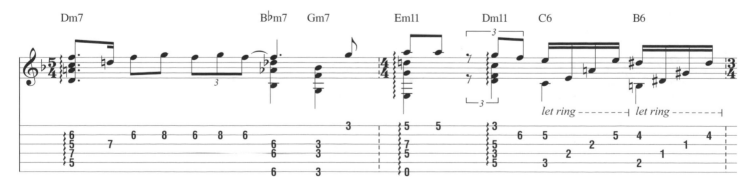

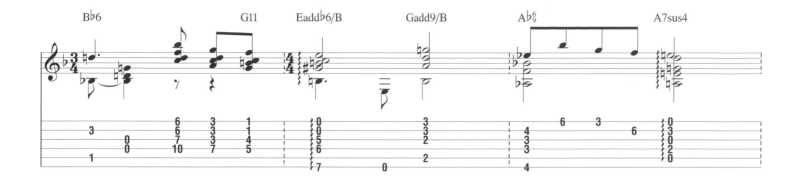

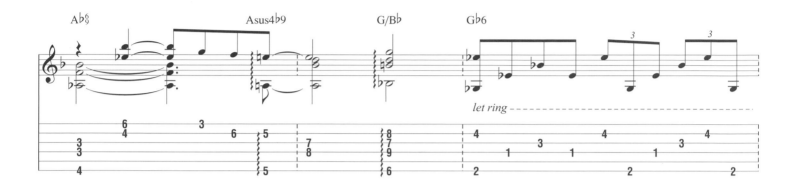

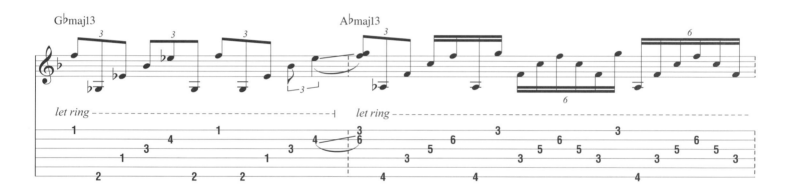

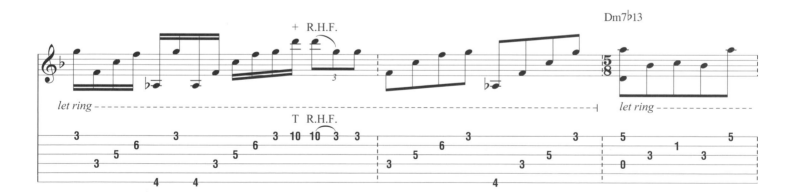

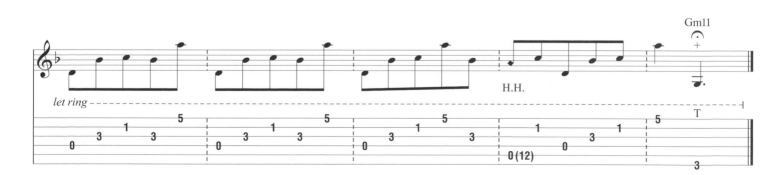

Prelude to a Kiss

Words by Irving Gordon and Irving Mills
Music by Duke Ellington

*Chord symbols reflect implied harmony.

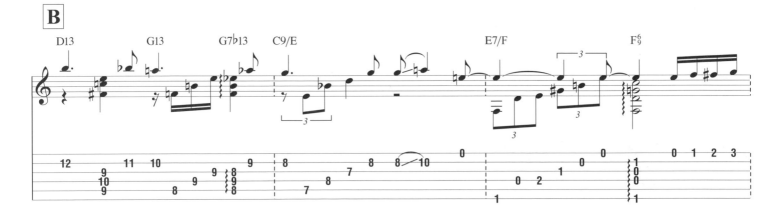

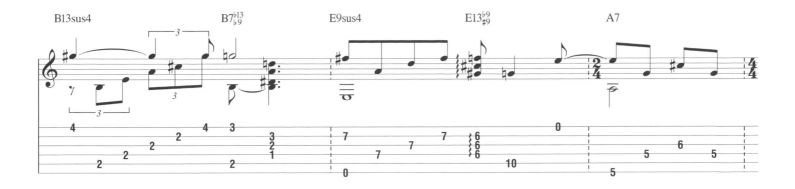

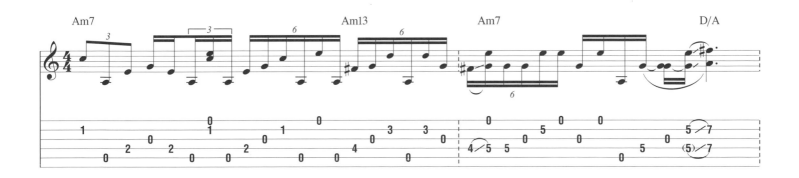

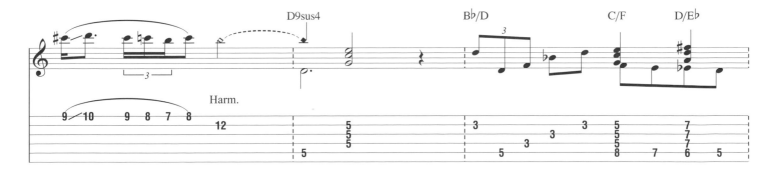

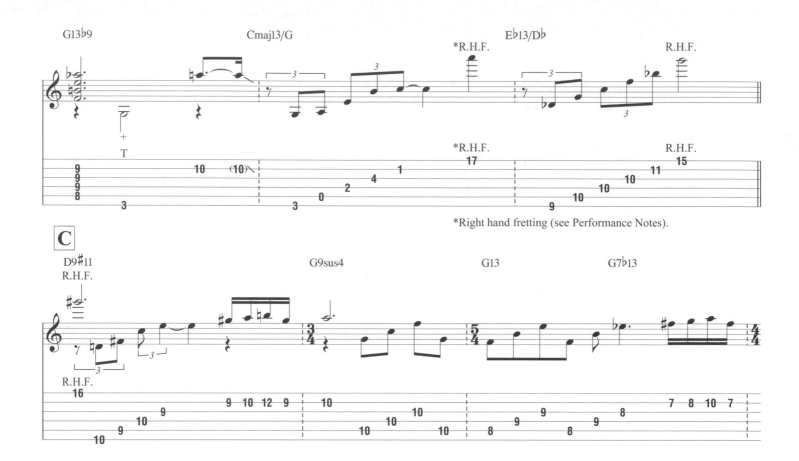

*Right hand fretting (see Performance Notes).

C

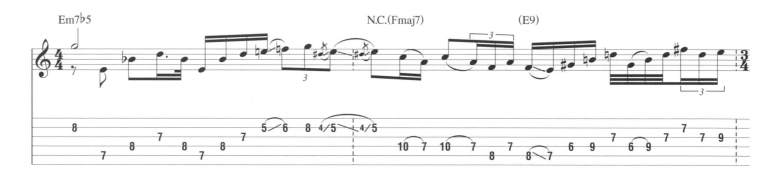

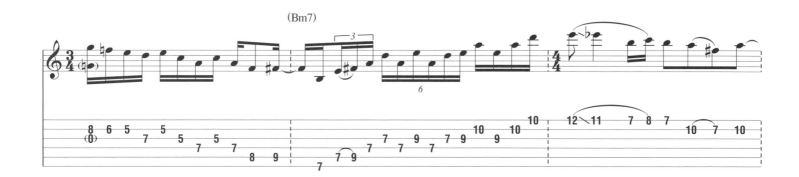

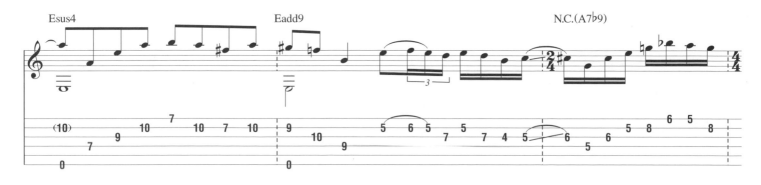

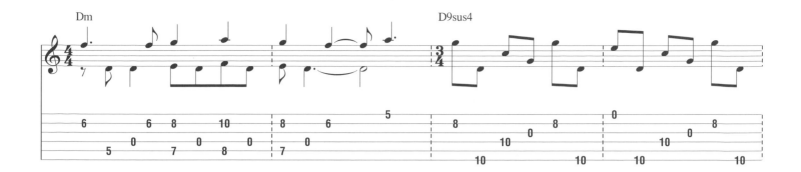

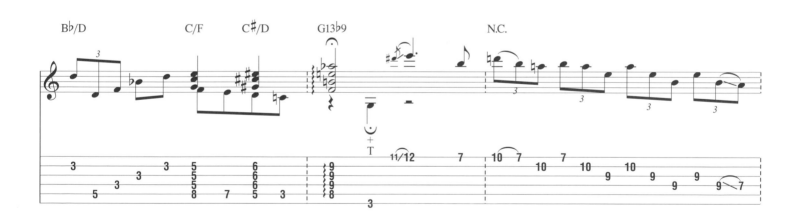

D

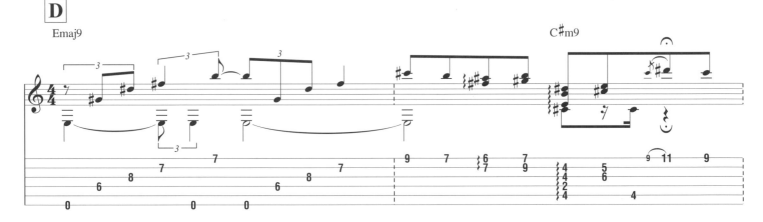

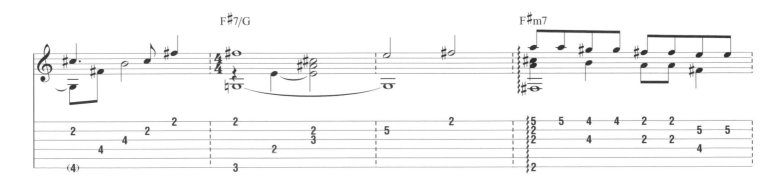

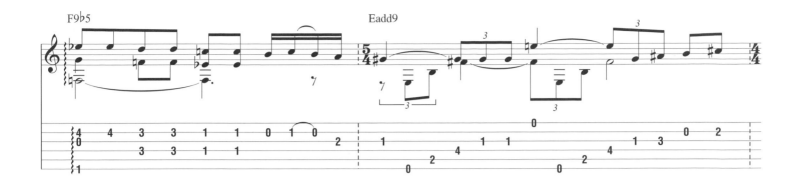

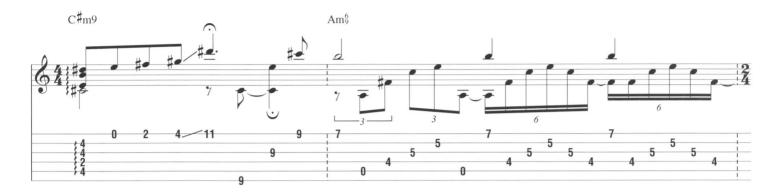

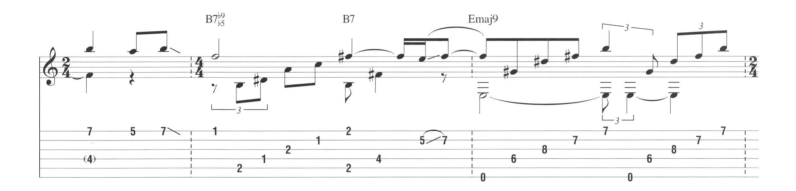

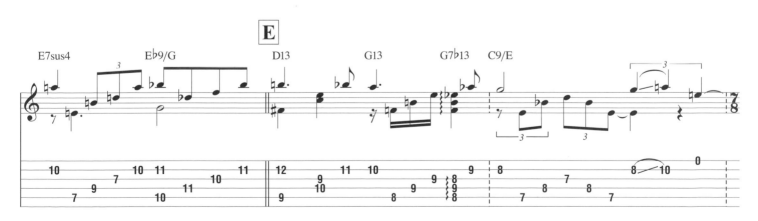

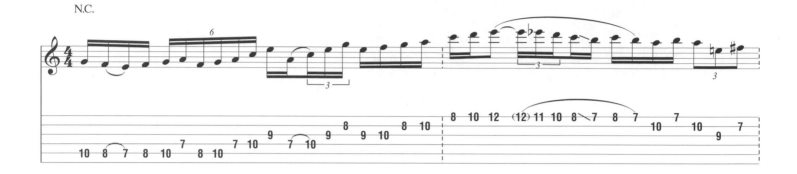

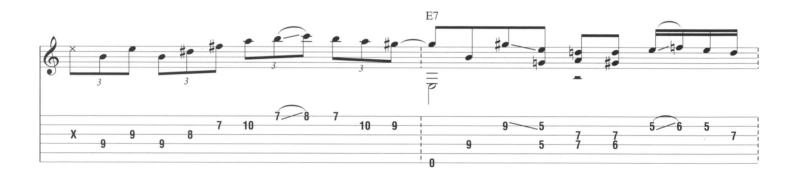

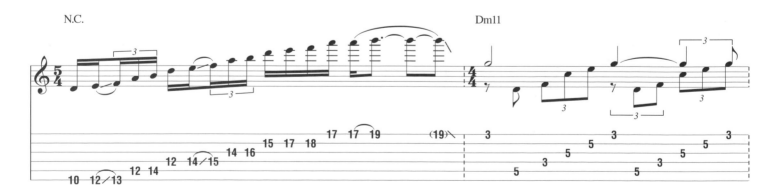

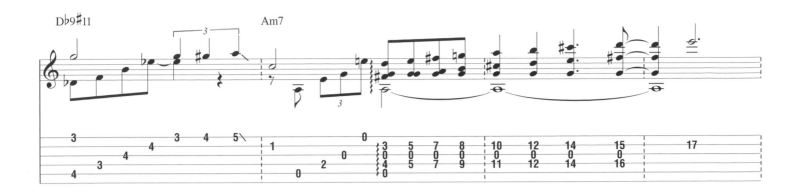

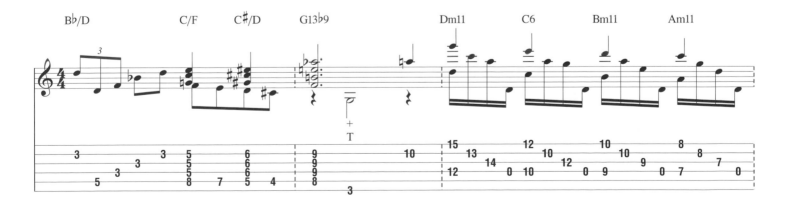

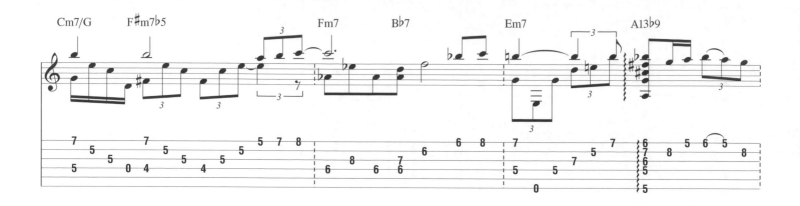

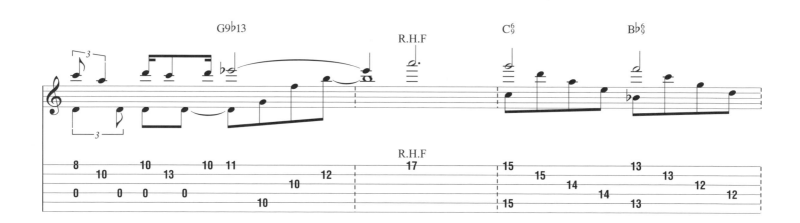

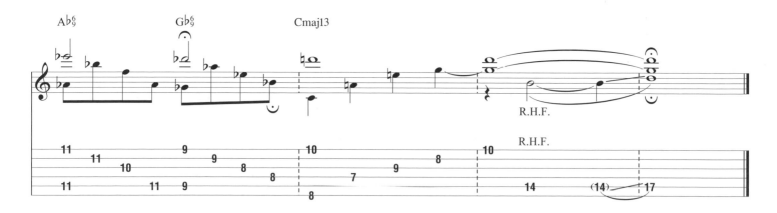

There Will Never Be Another You

from the Motion Picture ICELAND

Lyric by Mack Gordon
Music by Harry Warren

*Chord symbols reflect implied harmony.

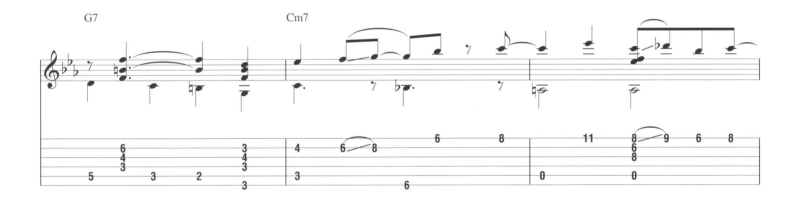

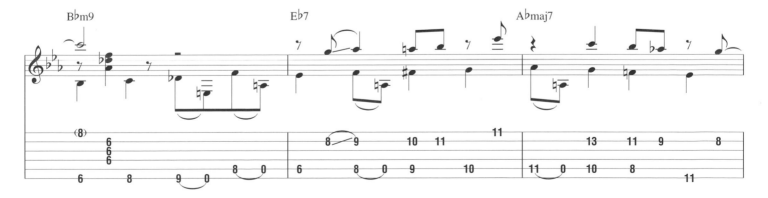

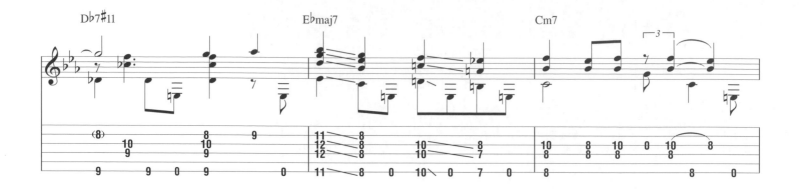

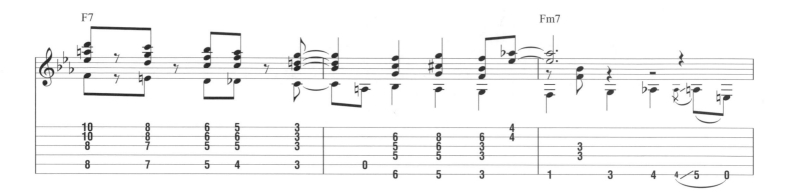

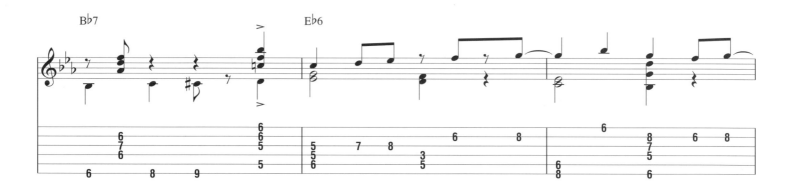

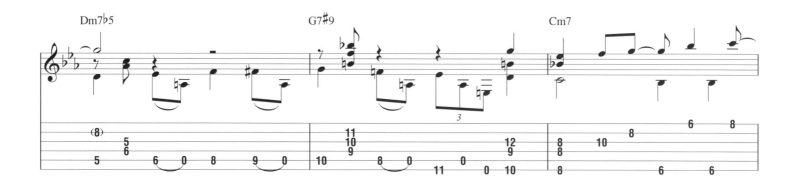

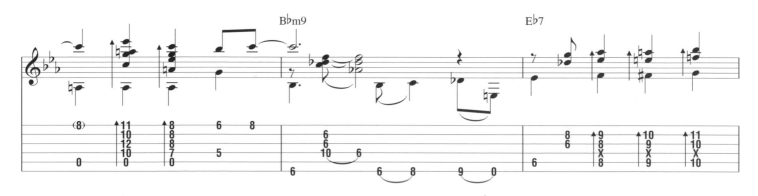

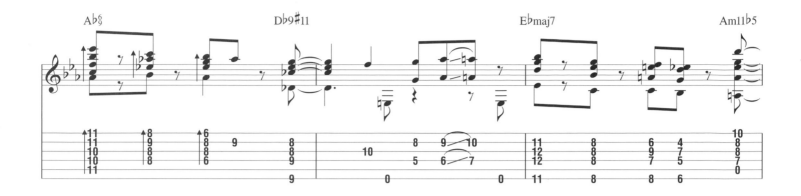

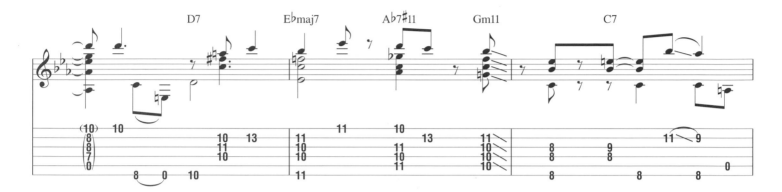

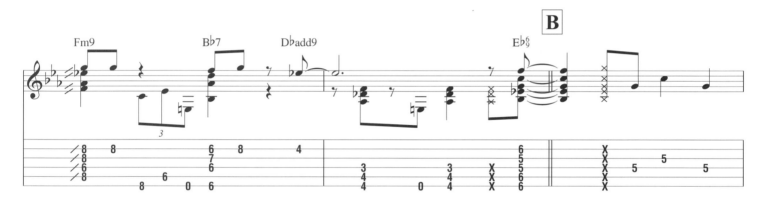

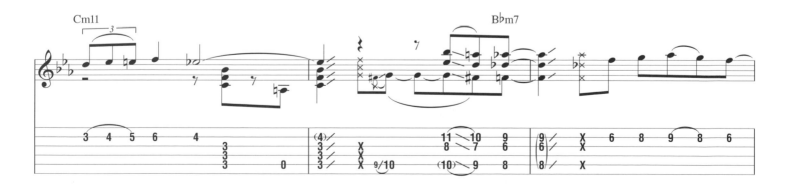

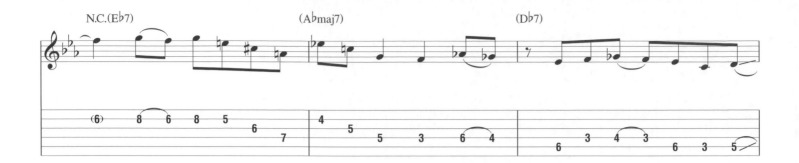

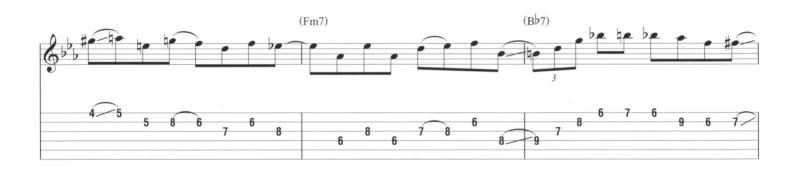

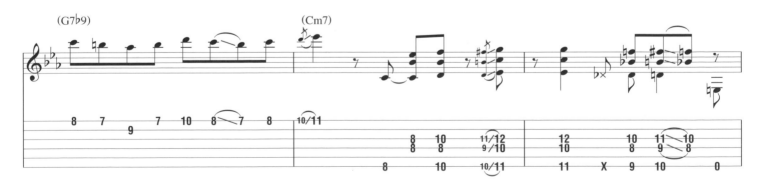

94

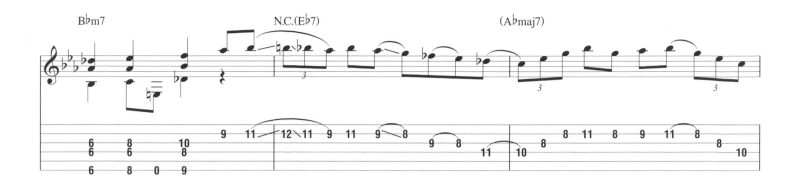

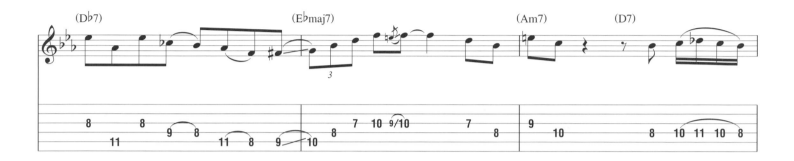

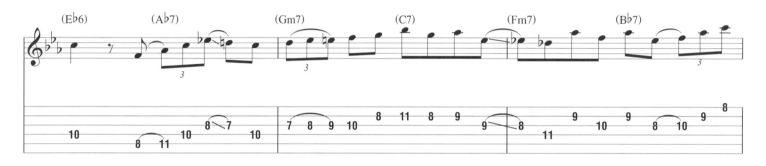

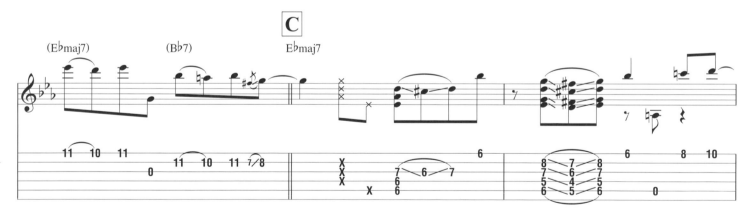

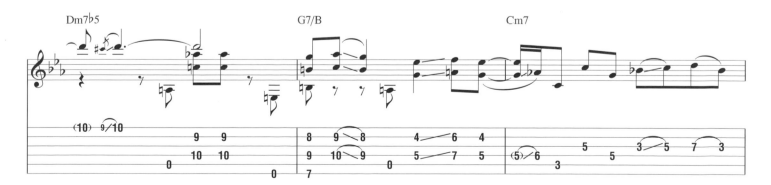

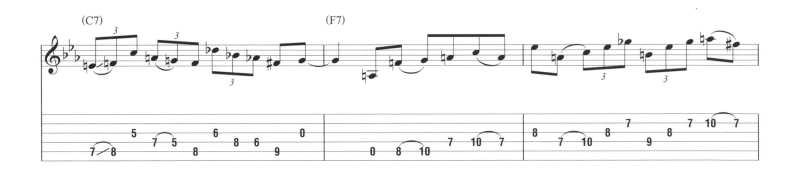

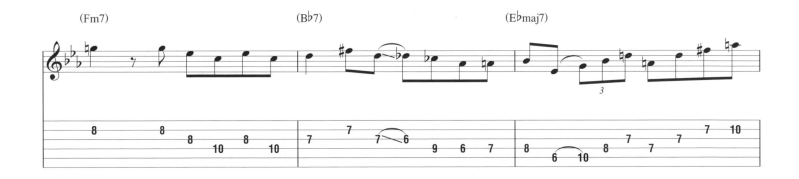

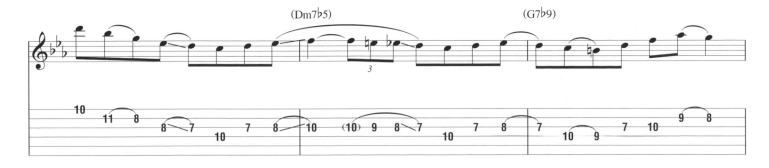

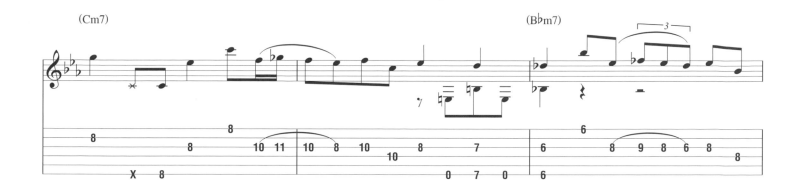

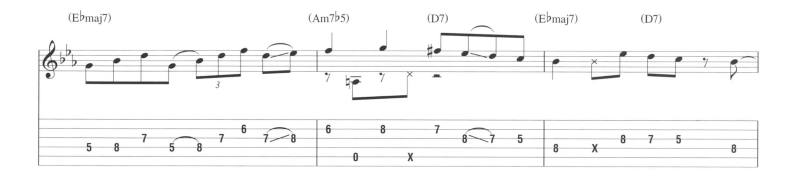

D

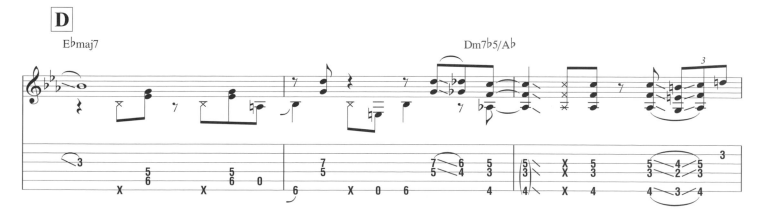

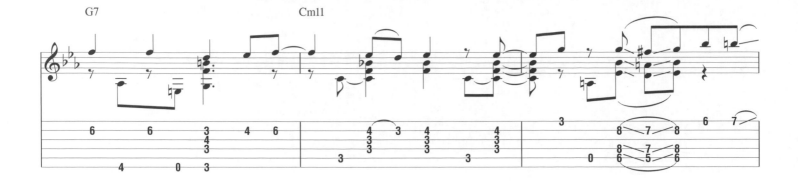

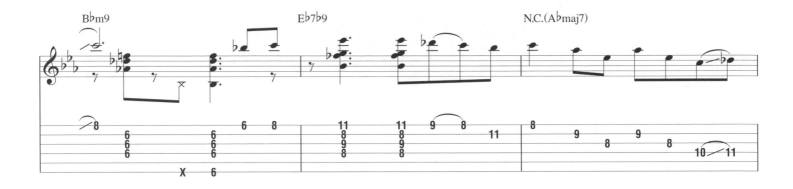

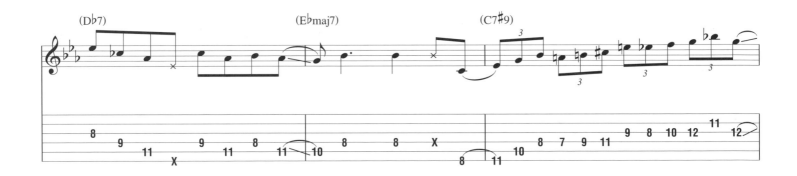

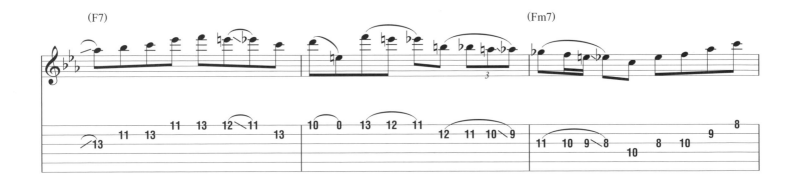

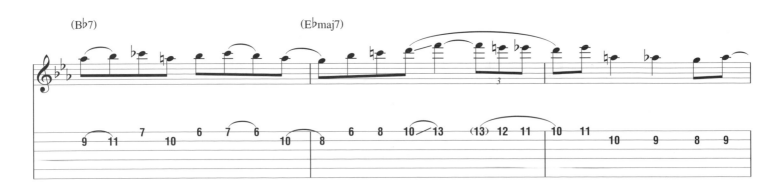

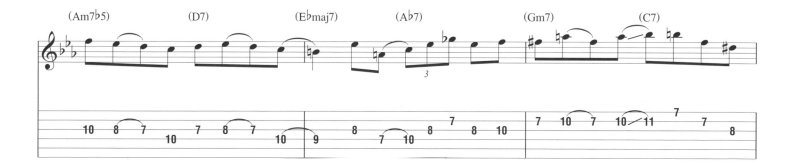

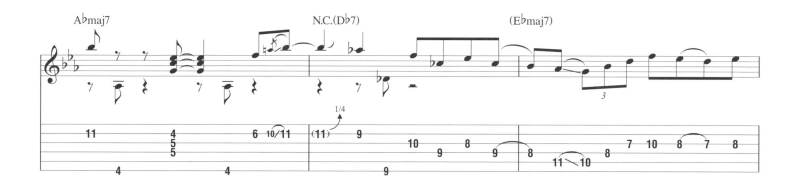

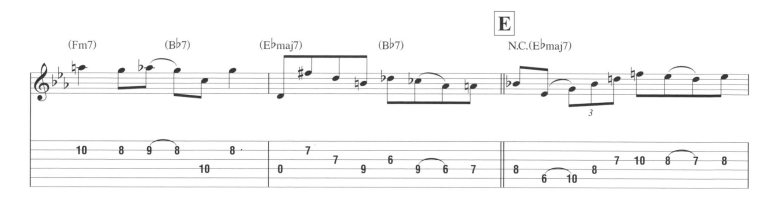

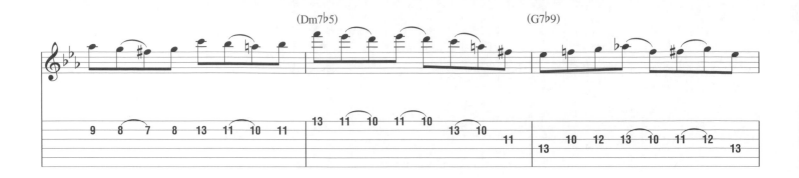

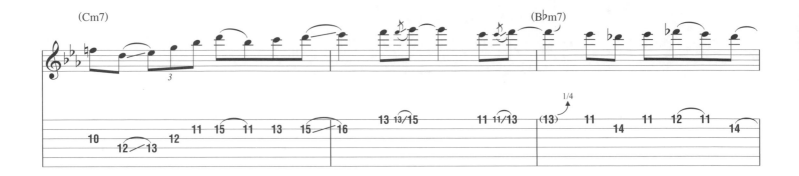

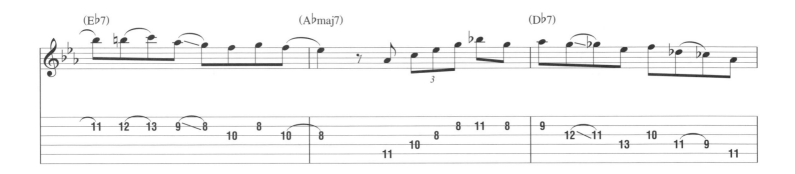

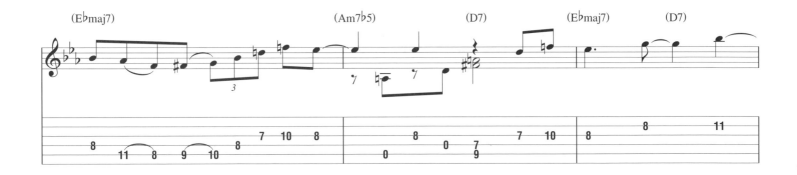

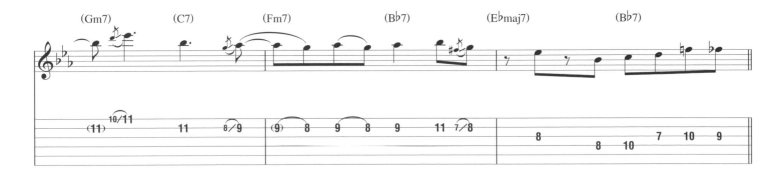

F

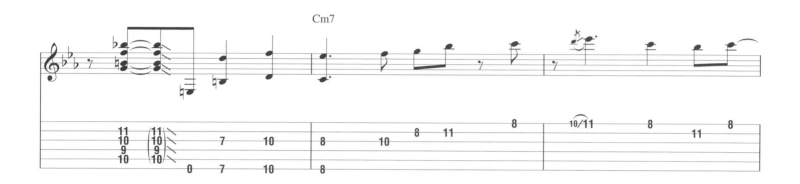

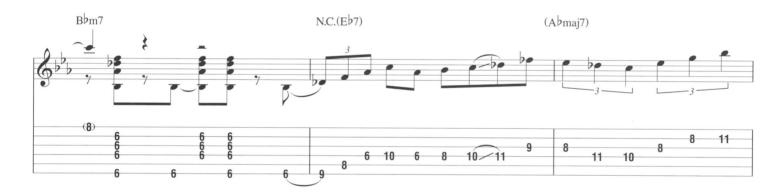

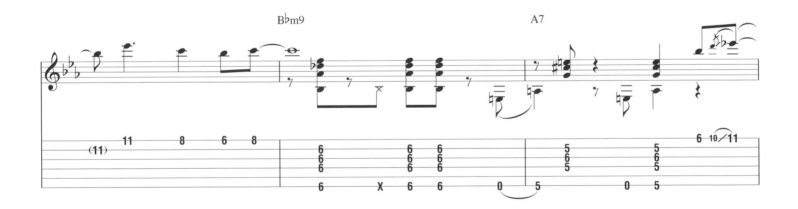

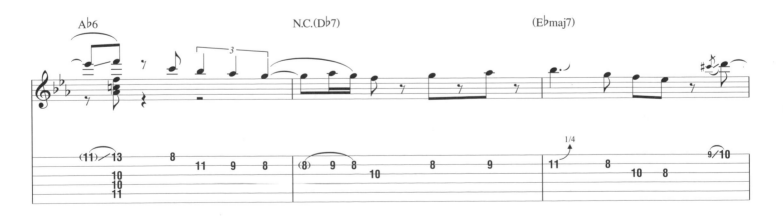

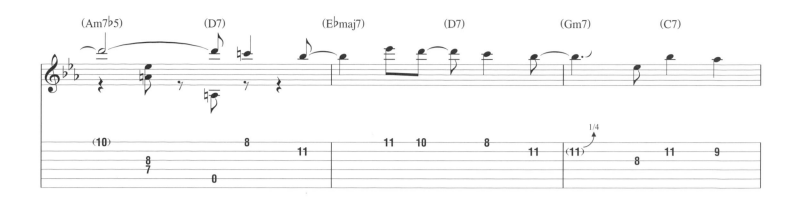

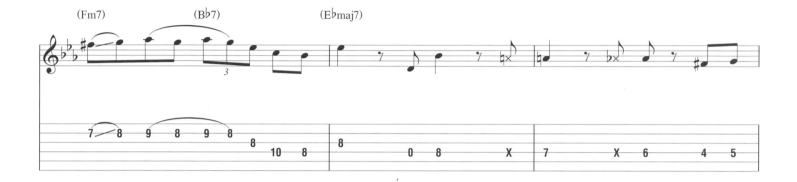

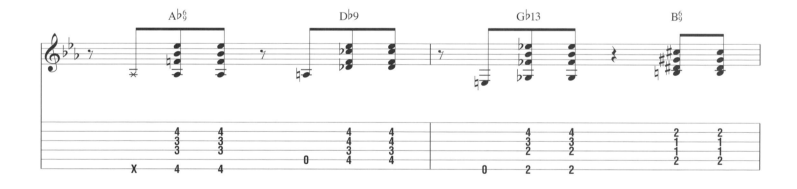

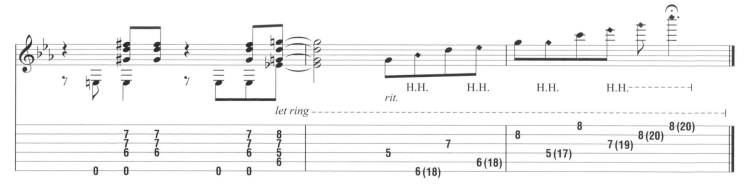

Ruby, My Dear

By Thelonious Monk

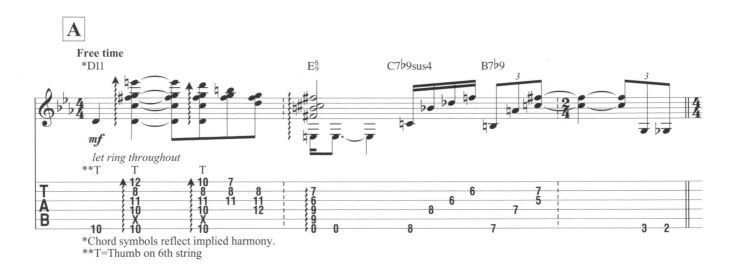

*Chord symbols reflect implied harmony.
**T=Thumb on 6th string

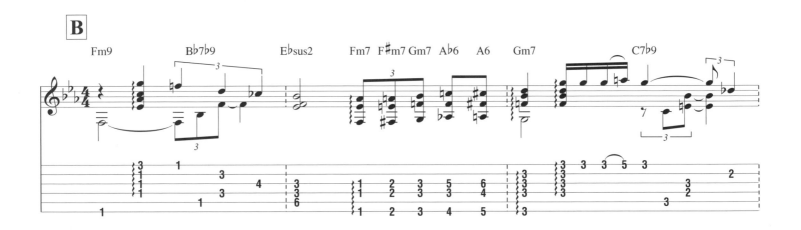

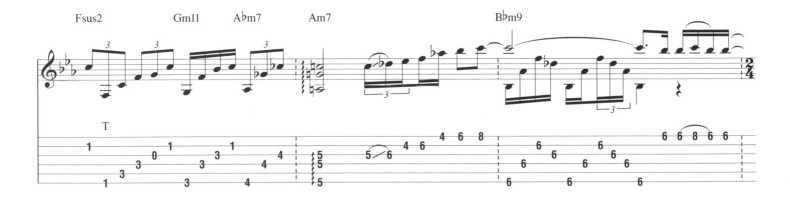

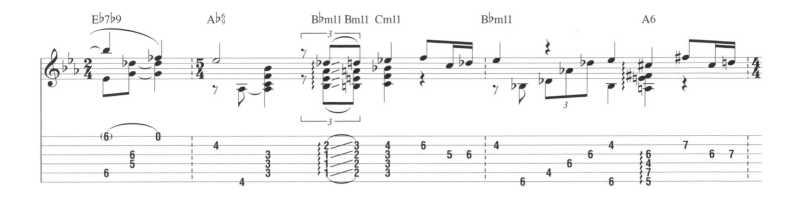

*Right hand fretting (see Performance Notes).

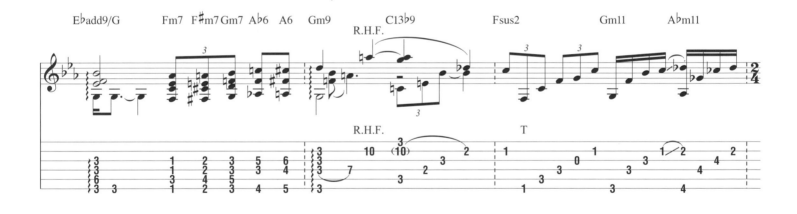

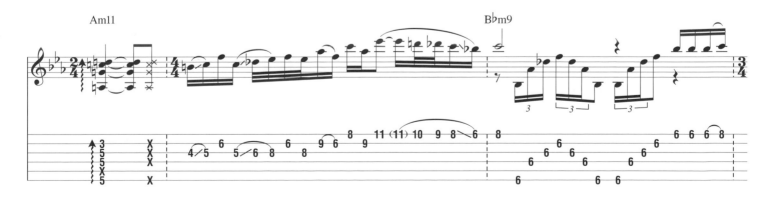

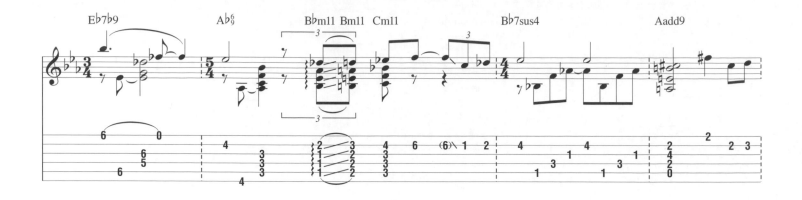

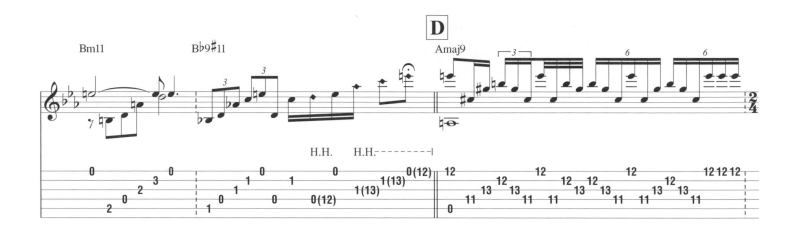

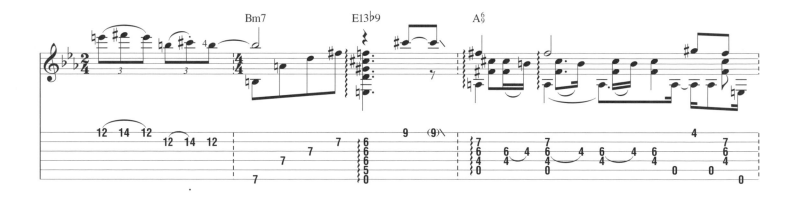

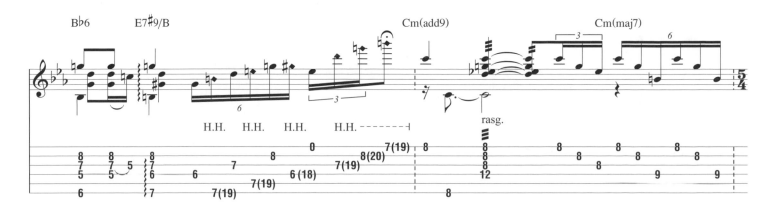

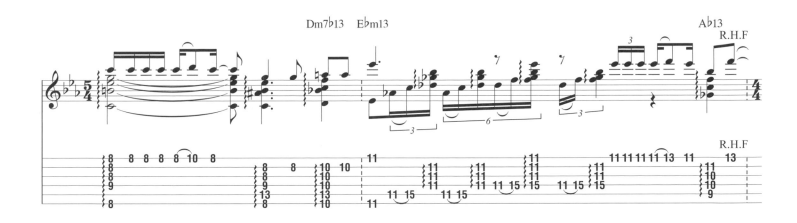

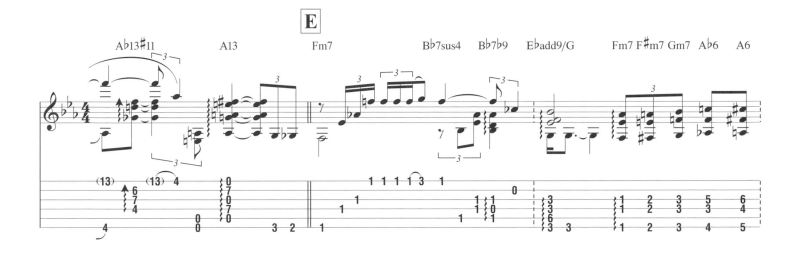

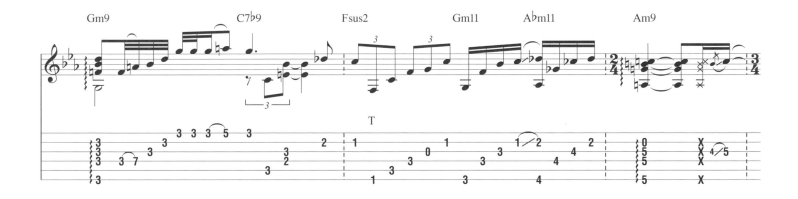

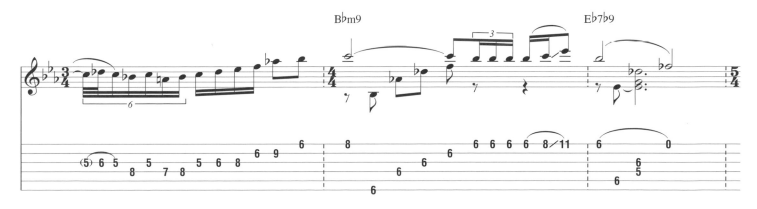

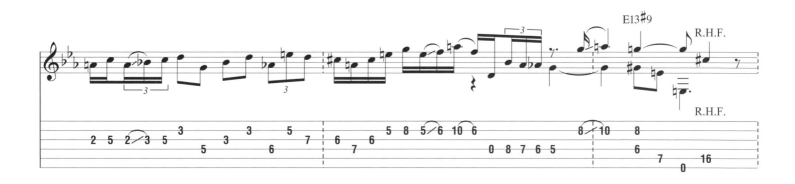

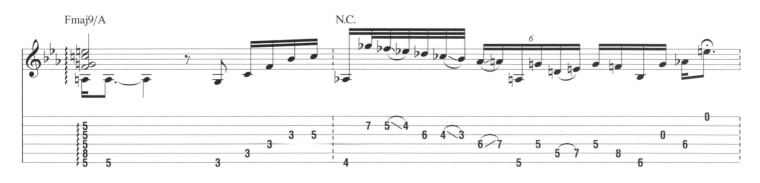

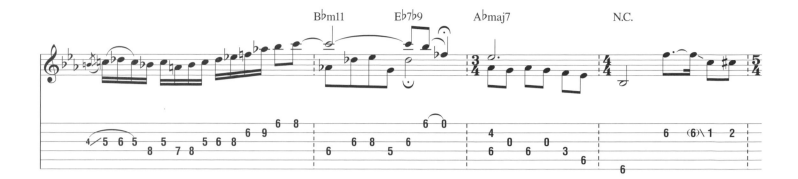

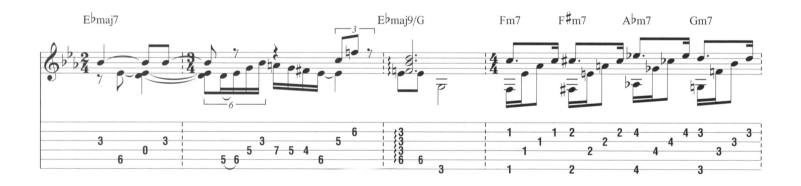

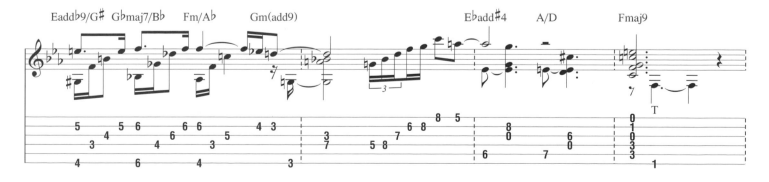

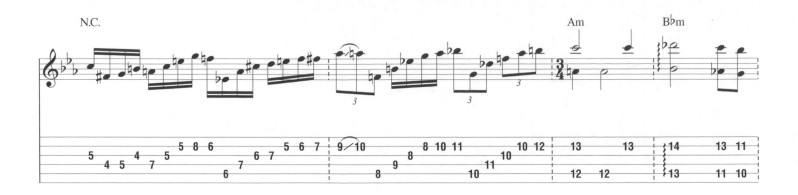

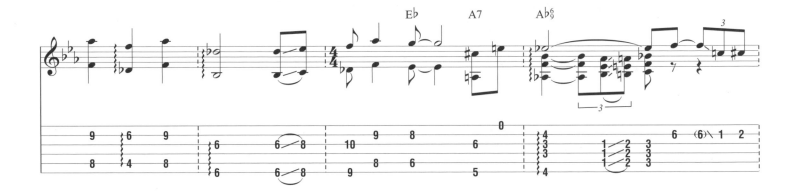

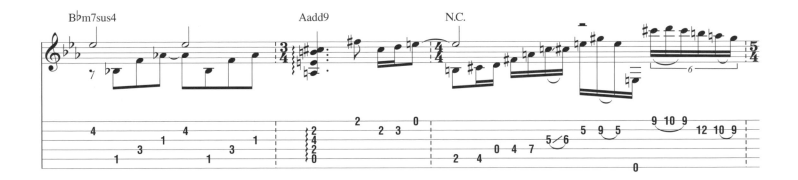

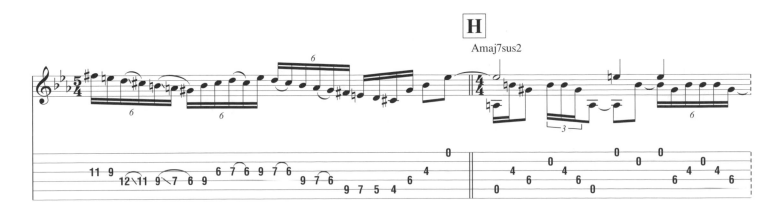

110

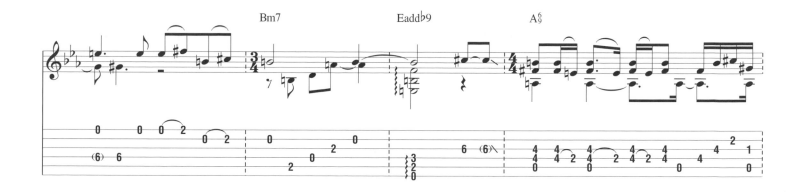

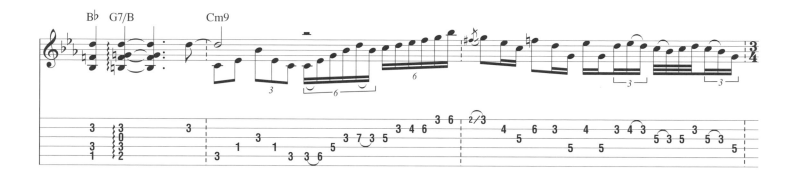

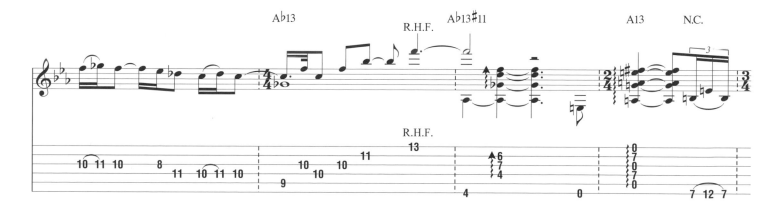

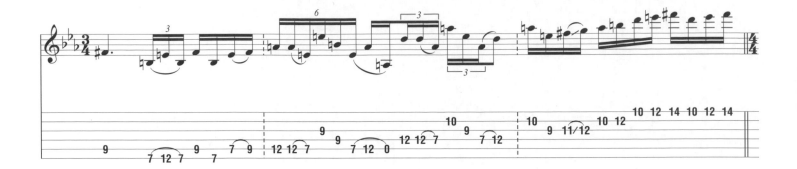

I

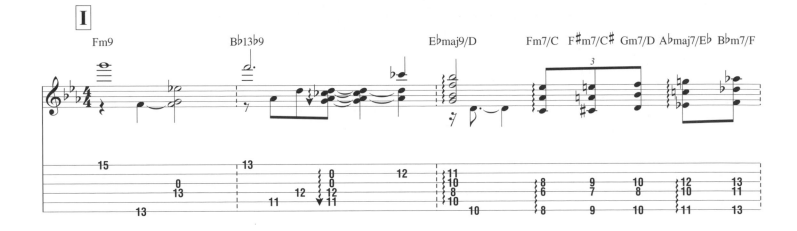

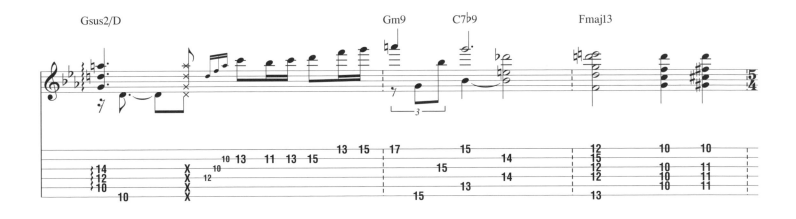

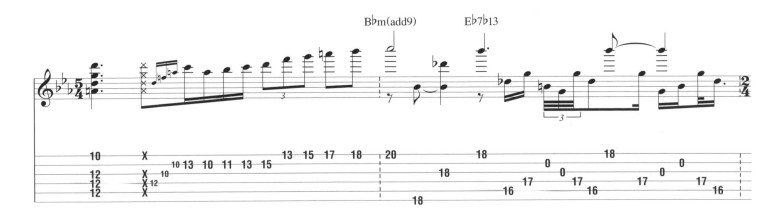

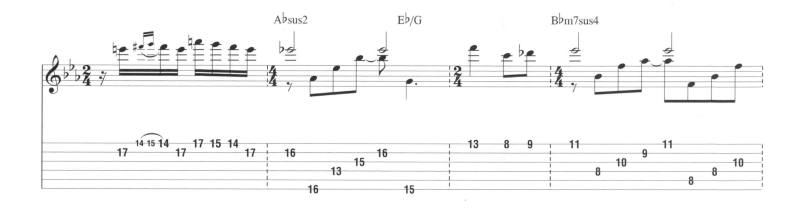

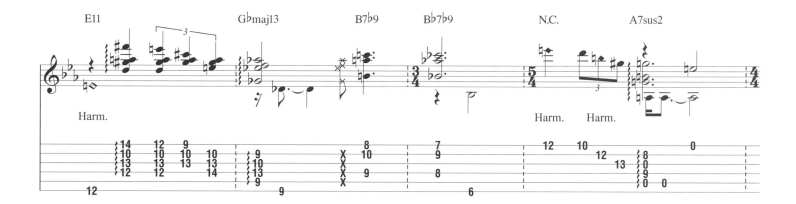

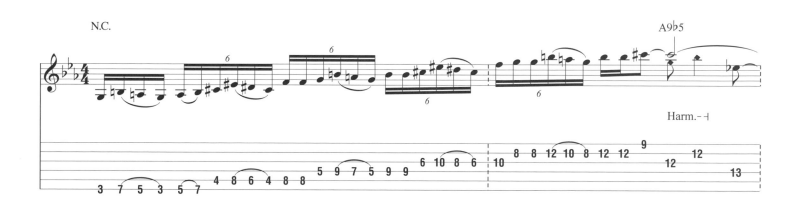

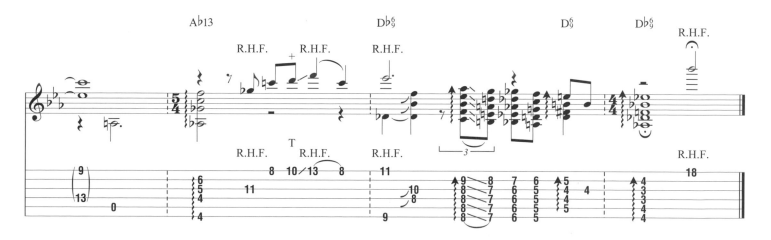

Stolen Moments

Words and Music by Oliver Nelson

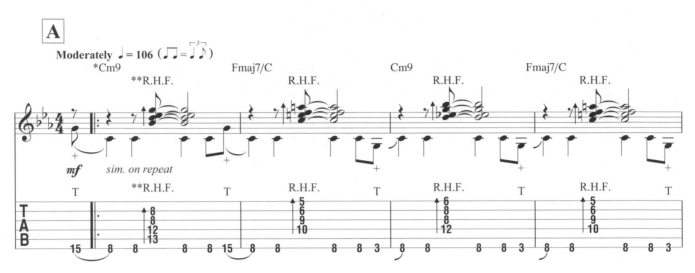

*Chord symbols reflect implied harmony.
**Right hand fretting (see Performance Notes), lowest
note of upstem chords only (next 8 meas.).

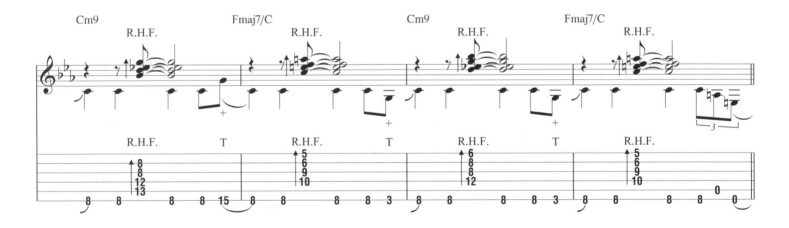

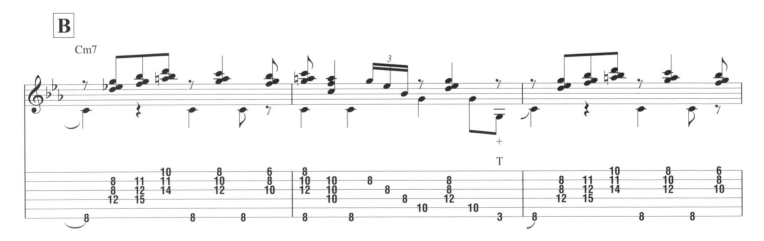

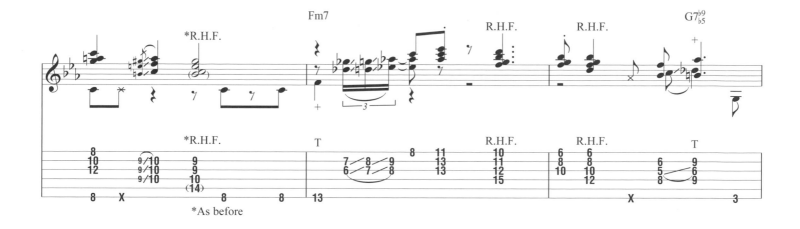

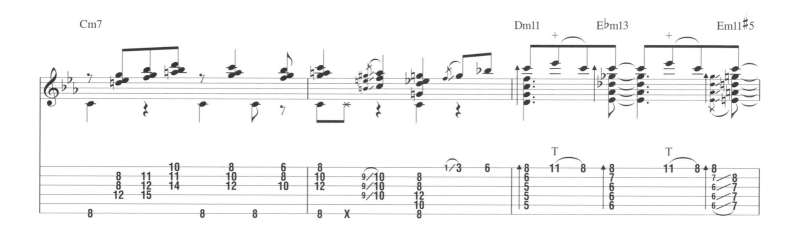

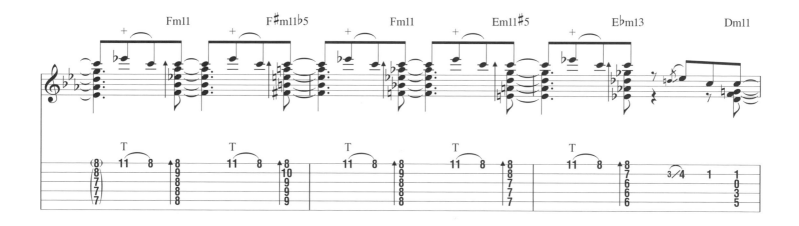

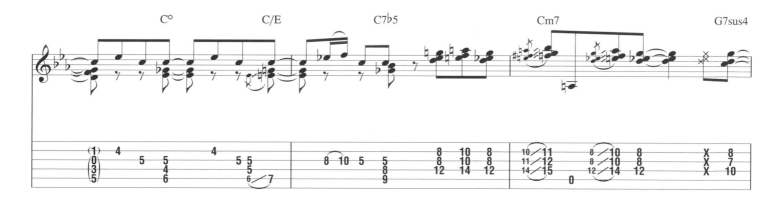

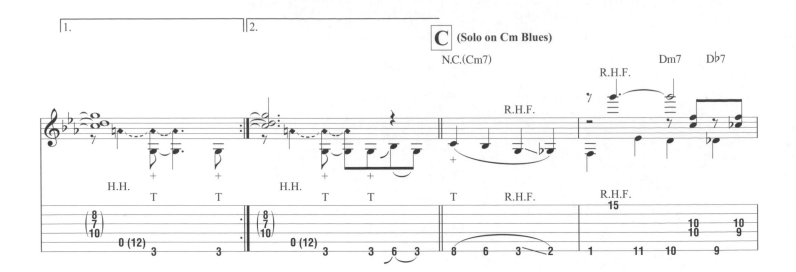

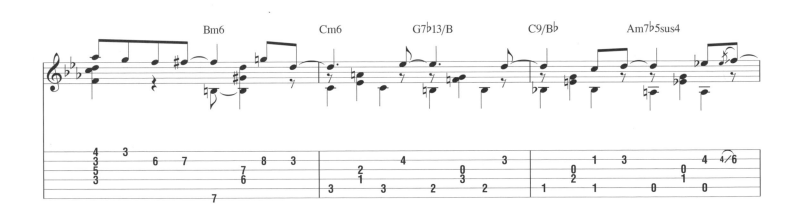

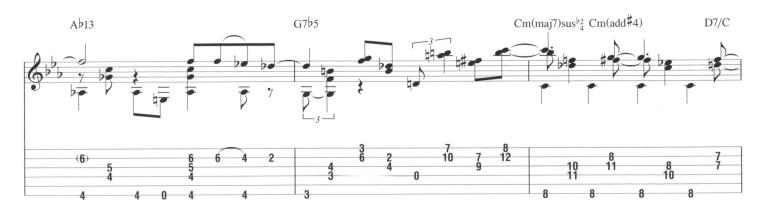

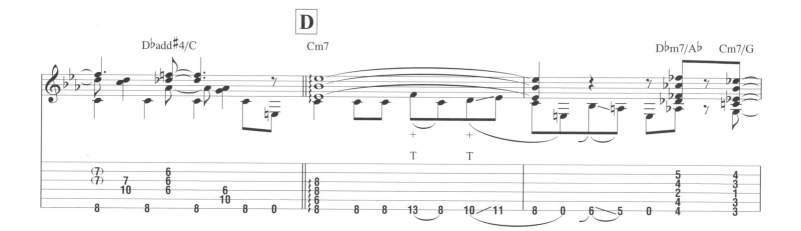

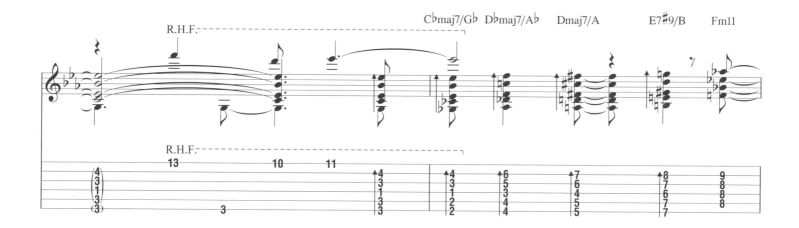

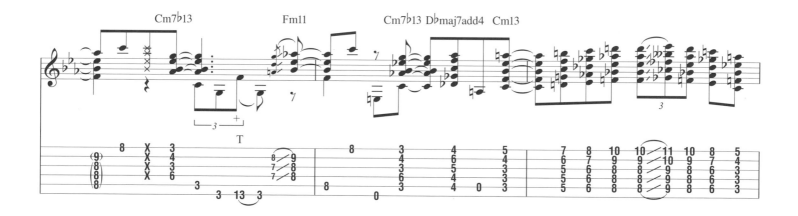

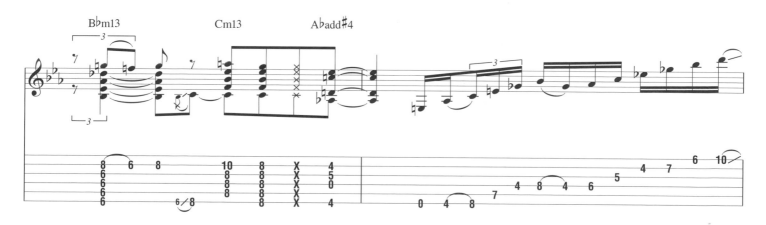

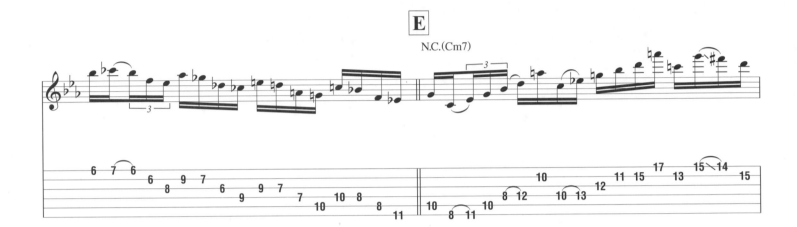

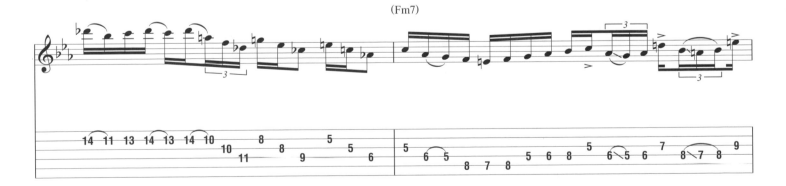

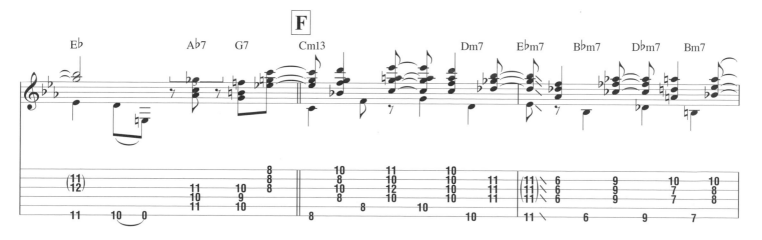

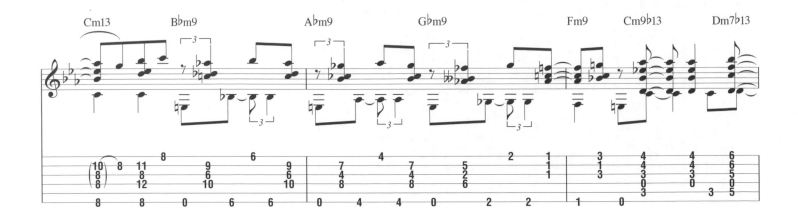

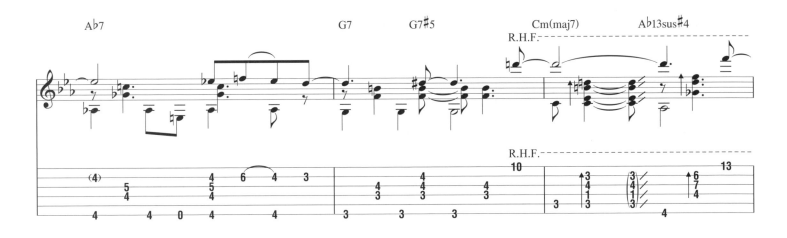

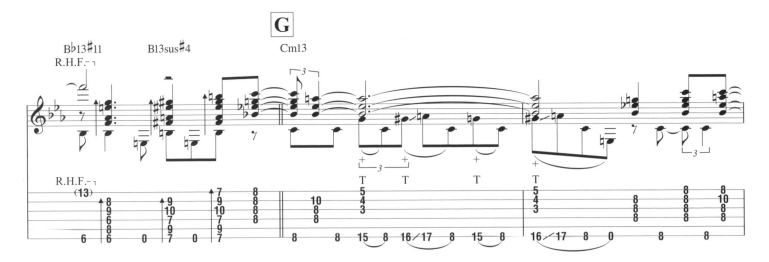

D7   D♭7   Cm13

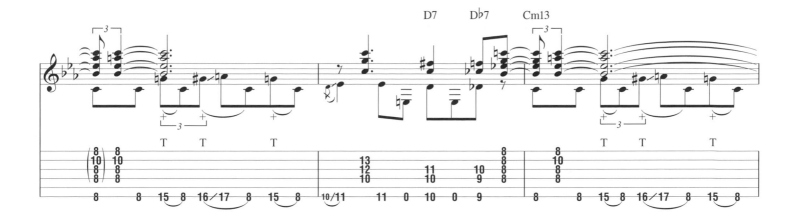

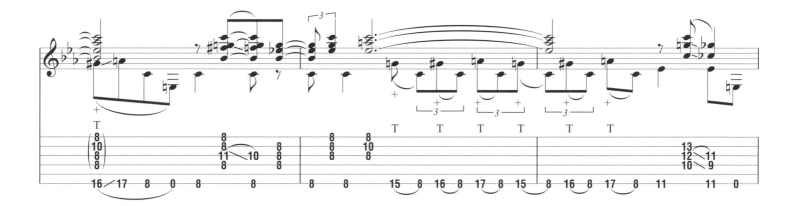

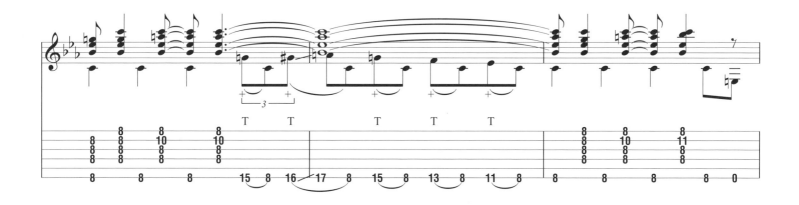

*Faster ♩ = 159
Cm   Fadd$^9_4$ *Repeat and fade*

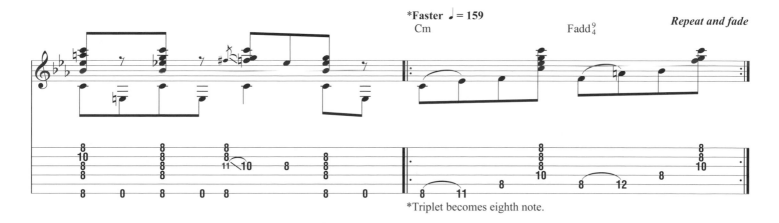

*Triplet becomes eighth note.

Where or When

from BABES IN ARMS
Words by Lorenz Hart
Music by Richard Rodgers

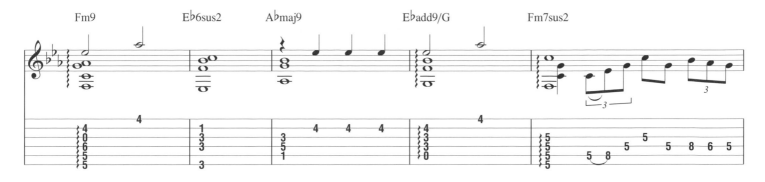

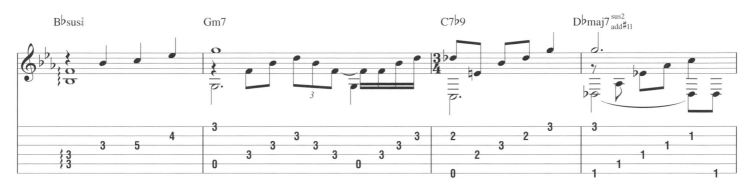

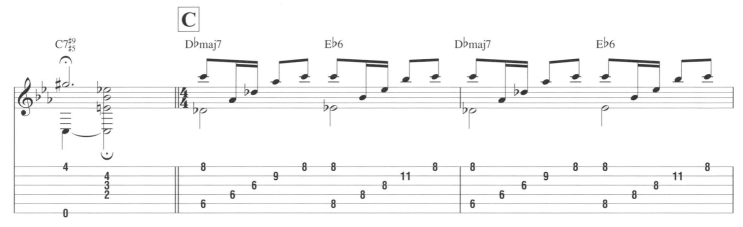

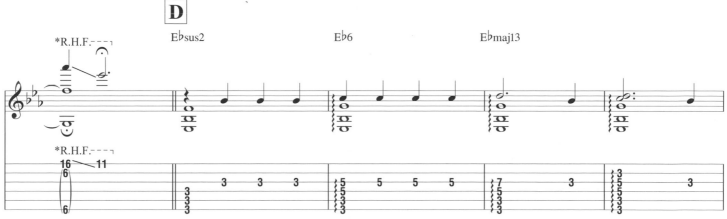

*Right hand fretting (see Performance Notes).

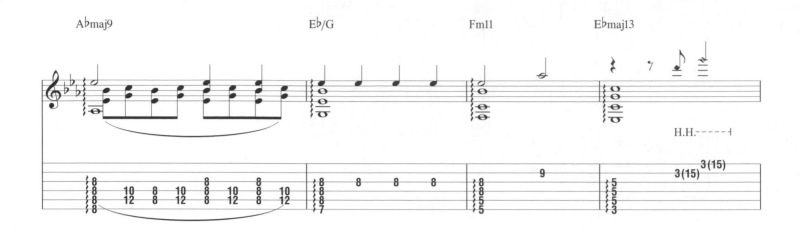

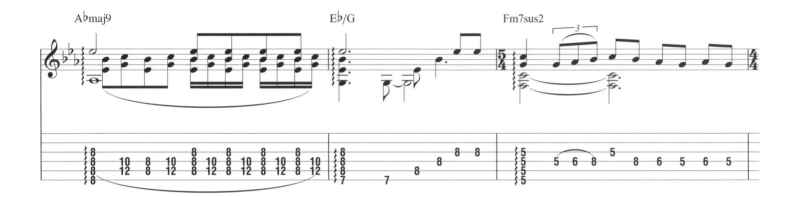

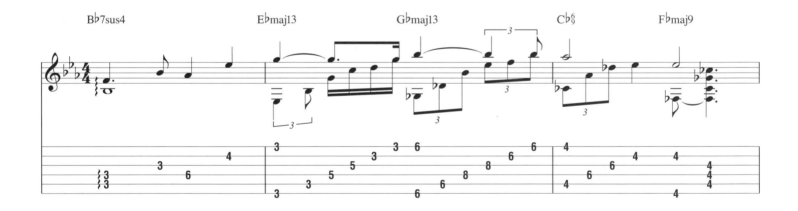

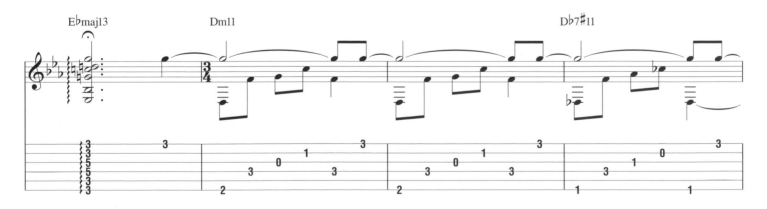

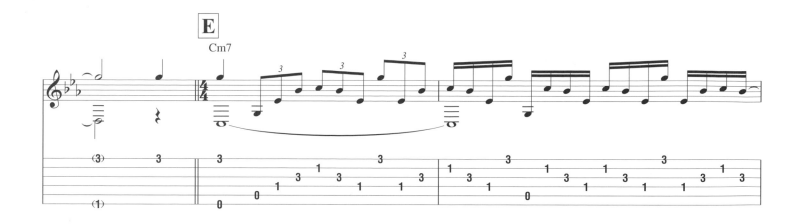

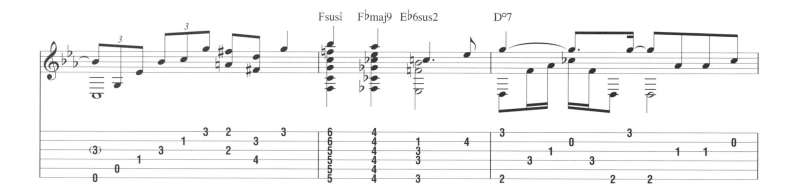

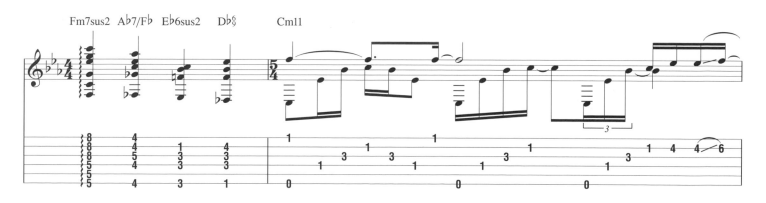

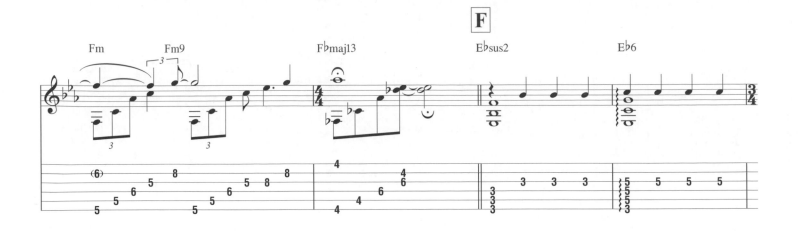

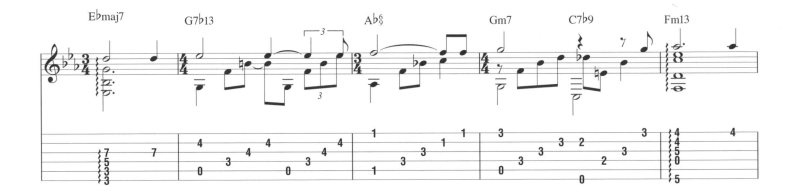

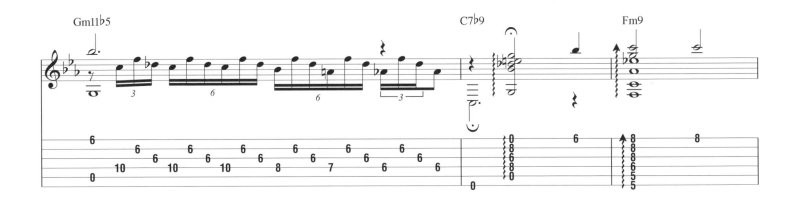

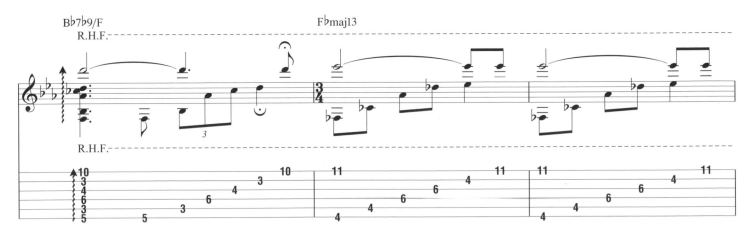

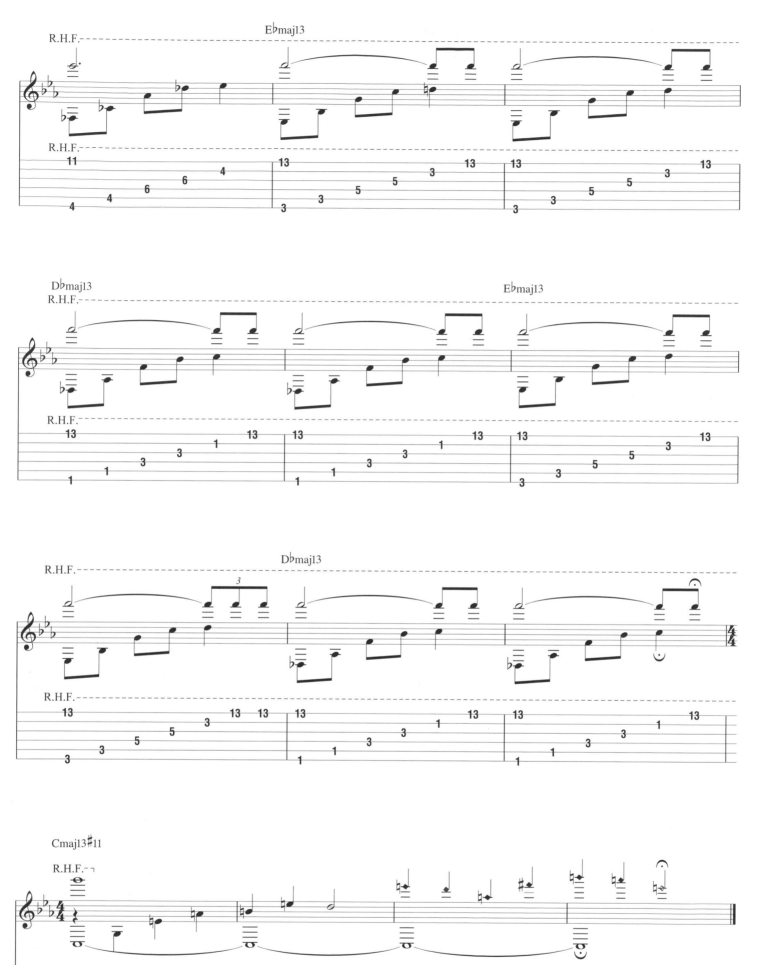

JAZZ GUITAR CHORD MELODY SOLOS

This series features chord melody arrangements in standard notation and tablature of songs for intermediate guitarists.

ALL-TIME STANDARDS

27 songs, including: All of Me • Bewitched • Come Fly with Me • A Fine Romance • Georgia on My Mind • How High the Moon • I'll Never Smile Again • I've Got You Under My Skin • It's De-Lovely • It's Only a Paper Moon • My Romance • Satin Doll • The Surrey with the Fringe on Top • Yesterdays • and more.
00699757 Solo Guitar.....................$14.99

IRVING BERLIN

27 songs, including: Alexander's Ragtime Band • Always • Blue Skies • Cheek to Cheek • Easter Parade • Happy Holiday • Heat Wave • How Deep Is the Ocean • Puttin' On the Ritz • Remember • They Say It's Wonderful • What'll I Do? • White Christmas • and more.
00700637 Solo Guitar.....................$14.99

CHRISTMAS CAROLS

26 songs, including: Auld Lang Syne • Away in a Manger • Deck the Hall • God Rest Ye Merry, Gentlemen • Good King Wenceslas • Here We Come A-Wassailing • It Came upon the Midnight Clear • Joy to the World • O Holy Night • O Little Town of Bethlehem • Silent Night • Toyland • We Three Kings of Orient Are • and more.
00701697 Solo Guitar.....................$12.99

CHRISTMAS JAZZ

21 songs, including Auld Lang Syne • Baby, It's Cold Outside • Cool Yule • Have Yourself a Merry Little Christmas • I've Got My Love to Keep Me Warm • Mary, Did You Know? • Santa Baby • Sleigh Ride • White Christmas • Winter Wonderland • and more.
00171334 Solo Guitar.....................$14.99

DISNEY SONGS

27 songs, including: Beauty and the Beast • Can You Feel the Love Tonight • Candle on the Water • Colors of the Wind • A Dream Is a Wish Your Heart Makes • Heigh-Ho • Some Day My Prince Will Come • Under the Sea • When You Wish upon a Star • A Whole New World (Aladdin's Theme) • Zip-A-Dee-Doo-Dah • and more.
00701902 Solo Guitar.....................$14.99

DUKE ELLINGTON

25 songs, including: C-Jam Blues • Caravan • Do Nothin' Till You Hear from Me • Don't Get Around Much Anymore • I Got It Bad and That Ain't Good • I'm Just a Lucky So and So • In a Sentimental Mood • It Don't Mean a Thing (If It Ain't Got That Swing) • Mood Indigo • Perdido • Prelude to a Kiss • Satin Doll • and more.
00700636 Solo Guitar.....................$12.99

FAVORITE STANDARDS

27 songs, including: All the Way • Autumn in New York • Blue Skies • Cheek to Cheek • Don't Get Around Much Anymore • How Deep Is the Ocean • I'll Be Seeing You • Isn't It Romantic? • It Could Happen to You • The Lady Is a Tramp • Moon River • Speak Low • Take the "A" Train • Willow Weep for Me • Witchcraft • and more.
00699756 Solo Guitar.....................$14.99

JAZZ BALLADS

27 songs, including: Body and Soul • Darn That Dream • Easy to Love (You'd Be So Easy to Love) • Here's That Rainy Day • In a Sentimental Mood • Misty • My Foolish Heart • My Funny Valentine • The Nearness of You • Stella by Starlight • Time After Time • The Way You Look Tonight • When Sunny Gets Blue • and more.
00699755 Solo Guitar.....................$14.99

LATIN STANDARDS

27 Latin favorites, including: Água De Beber (Water to Drink) • Desafinado • The Girl from Ipanema • How Insensitive (Insensatez) • Little Boat • Meditation • One Note Samba (Samba De Uma Nota So) • Poinciana • Quiet Nights of Quiet Stars • Samba De Orfeu • So Nice (Summer Samba) • Wave • and more.
00699754 Solo Guitar.....................$14.99

Prices, content, and availability subject to change without notice.
Disney characters and artwork ©Disney Enterprises, Inc.